Driftboats

A Complete Guide

Dan Alsup

Driftboats

PATRICK FARRELL

A Complete Guide

Dan Alsup

Frank
Amato
PORTLAND

DANIELLE MARIE ALSUP

This book is dedicated to the boatmen whose
love of running swift and wild rivers
led to the creation and perfecting
of the little riverboats
known as driftboats.

Frank Amato Publications, Inc.
P.O. Box 82112, Portland, Oregon 97282
503•653•8108 www.amatobooks.com
Cover illustration by Keith McGuire; photographed by Jim Schollmeyer
All photographs by Dan Alsup unless otherwise noted.
Book and Cover Design: Kathy Johnson
Printed in Hong Kong
ISBN: 1-57188-189-1   UPC: 0-66066-00400-0
1 3 5 7 9 10 8 6 4 2

Table of Contents

Prince and Marjorie Helfrich, happy partners in adventure.

COURTESY OF ROY PRUITT

Vic Lansaw and Rick Alsup on the Rogue.

Fish on!

COURTESY OF LAVRO BOATS

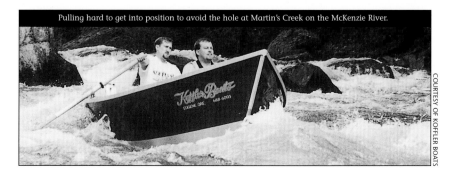

Pulling hard to get into position to avoid the hole at Martin's Creek on the McKenzie River.

COURTESY OF KOFFLER BOATS

Acknowledgments

Many, many people made numerous contributions to this book, especially to the historical research. Delving into the history of the driftboat has been an adventure unto itself. The research process behind this book was rewarding in and of itself as I met and made so many new friends and acquaintances. I will try to include everyone that has contributed time for interviews, photographs, and editing time. I sincerely thank everyone for his or her time and efforts towards making this book a reality.

In alphabetical order: Donna Alsup, my gorgeous wife who put up with my many late hours and helped type the manuscript, she knew that it would never end, I would never finish this; Danielle Alsup, my lovely daughter who drew the driftboat picture; Rick Alsup, my brother who accompanied me on many of my research and photography expeditions; Laurie Alsup, my sister who helped with editing and proofreading; Frank Amato, the publisher who gave me the green light; Mark Angel, who opened his home and spent an afternoon with me providing his insights, photos, and the opportunities to take some photos of boats he had raised from the bottom of the Deschutes River; Florence Arman, for her encouragement, permission to quote from her book, and the use of her photographs; Dennis Belles, co-owner of Clackamas Marine for his friendship, his insights, photographs and for steering me towards some very interesting research leads; Bruce Bergstrom of Sawyer Oars. Bruce was more than helpful and generous with his time to answered my many questions; Eric Bigler, Deschutes River guide whose enthusiasm for river running encouraged my first real whitewater adventure and for the photos he provided; Karen Bigler for the great duct tape story; Scott Davis, for his help with my computer system that enabled me to finish this project; Roger Fletcher of The River's Touch. Roger was a great encourager who gave generously to this project. He very unselfishly shared his research with me. He also pointed me towards some very interesting sources. His scale models of the historic early driftboats really brought to life the evolution of the driftboat; Ron Gifford, my friend and fishing companion, without whom I may never have ventured forth in a driftboat.; Ray Heater and Cy Happy of Ray's River Dories. These two gentlemen do a wonderful job of keeping alive the art of building outstanding wooden driftboats, particularly the Rapid Robert and Rogue River style driftboats. Ray also helped by proofreading the manuscript for content; Lee Haslet, my very good friend who has provided invaluable help with editing and computer work. Lee also accompanied me on some of my research trips. Lee, I miss you a lot now that you've moved to Iderhoe, my best to you always; Dave Helfrich, who kindly answered my questions about his father, Prince, and his recollections of the early driftboats; Don Hill, both guide and driftboat builder, Don was a great encourager and provider of historical information and photos; Willie Illingsworth, who gave freely of his time answering my questions and reviewing portions of the manuscript. He provided the exciting photo of himself in the middle of Blossom Bar Rapid and gave permission to use his photo from one of his advertising pamphlets; Art Isrealson, a long-time riverman and oarsman, Art is a retired Firefighter from Gresham, Oregon, very active in the Northwest Steelheader's Association and the Northwest Rafter's Association. He reviewed the manuscript for accuracy of content; Kathryn Isrealson, Art's wife, reviewed my manuscript providing some good insight into its readability and helped edit out my many typos; Maurya Kaarhus generously opened her home to me for an afternoon. She read the portions of my manuscript concerning her grandfather, father and brother's involvement in the driftboat and offered some invaluable insights. She also provided some rare old photos; Ed Kammer and Rogue River Mailboats who provided the sailed mailboat photo to Curry County Historical Museum. Kenny King, a retired McKenzie guide and the first person to be inducted into the Fresh Water Fishing Hall of Fame. Kenny answered many questions about the early boats and provided some great historical photos; Ron Lavigueure, one of the owners/builders of Lavro fiberglass driftboats, who spent a couple of long-distance hours on the phone with me. He explained in detail the process of building a hand-laid fiberglass boat and provided some great pictures; Ray Nelson, college professor and communications consultant, as well as my cousin, took his time to review my manuscript. His comments, encouragements and criticisms were all very helpful and encouraging; Steve Pritchett provided some really nice photographs of Rogue River style boats that his father Bob Pritchett, built and the picture of the salmon trying to climb Rainy falls; Bob Pruitt, Rogue River fishing and Steens Mountain hunting guide. He ran over 800 trips down the Rogue before 1978. Bob spent some very interesting time with me on a couple of long distance phone conversations answering questions about the old days on the Rogue and sharing some interesting yarns with me; Leroy 'Roy' Pruitt, retired McKenzie fishing and Steens Mountain hunting guide. His father, Veltie Pruitt was responsible for one of he earliest McKenzie driftboat designs. No doubt his (Veltie's) collaboration with Tom Kaarhus on that first boat was instrumental in Tom's interest in pursuing the development of his original McKenzie River Driftboat/Rapid Robert. Roy gave generously of his time answering my questions. He spent one whole spring afternoon letting his chores go so he could go through his photo collection with me, telling me the story behind each one. He took the time to have copies made for me of many of his historical photos, as well as to review the manuscript of this book. Roy also took the time to explain the way he taught rowing to his university extension school students. One of the best parts of writing this book has been the new friends like Roy that I have come to know during this journey; Marty Rathje, successor to Woodie Hindman who kindly answered my questions; Dave Rodriguez reviewed some of my historical data and gave me the opportunity to photograph the old Woodie Hindman Rapid Robert. Dave also provided the photos of Prince Helfrich on the John Day River. Dave has a trove of information and artifacts from the early days as he would like to start a driftboater's museum; Bill Schmauch invited me to join his party on my second adventure down the Rogue. He reviewed the earliest version of my manuscript to give me some feedback on how I was doing. The positive feedback that he gave me was an inspiration to expand and finally complete this book; Jeff Sims, my brother helped me with my photography and computer problems. Vern Wimmer, of the Curry County Historical Museum for his help in securing the sail mailboat photo. *A very special thank you to all!*

Roy and Shelly Pruitt. Roy is the son of Veltie Pruitt—an early driftboating pioneer.

Introduction

DRIFTBOATS—ALSO CALLED MCKENZIE RIVER BOATS, Rogue River Specials, Rapid Roberts, square-enders, and double-enders—are a very unique river boat design. They were developed in Oregon by and for fishing guides, but their use has spread to recreational boaters and fishermen. These nimble boats were designed to negotiate the rocky shallows and treacherous rapids on the beautiful but rugged Rogue and McKenzie rivers. These boats evolved slowly from heavy logging boats and clumsy flat-bottomed row boats into the light-weight, highly maneuverable river dancers of today.

McKenzie guide Don Hill treating his wife, Wanda, and son, Kenny, to some great whitewater at Martin's Creek Rapid.

COURTESY OF DON HILL RIVER BOATS

A beautiful custom-crafted wooden McKenzie boat. Originally a kit from Don Hill, it was assembled, customized and finished by Dave Edwards.

DAVE EDWARDS

Usually between 13 and 18 feet long, driftboats have a unique shape as the bottom of the boat is upswept or curved at the bow and the stern. This feature is called rocker because it is curved like the rocker on a rocking chair. The features most people recognize when they see the boats in the river are their dory-like, raked (upswept) gunwales that give the hull its distinctive shape. Traditionally, they are measured around the hull from stem to stern instead of the straight-line measurement from stem to the stern used on other kinds of boats. (See diagram page 10) This came about because the first driftboats were made of continuous planks. If 16-foot planks were used, the boat was considered to be a 16-footer. If it was measured in a straight line from stem to stern, it would measure out a little shorter.

While the driftboat has traditionally been a rowed boat, it is operated a little differently than other row-boats. Normally, an oarsman rows with his back toward the bow, while rowing backwards towards a destination. He is forced to look over his shoulder to see where he is going or depend on someone else in the boat telling him where to go. When used on a fast river with many obstacles, it is not hard to see how awkward this style of rowing could be.

Driftboats are rowed (or lowered) downstream with the oarsman facing downstream as well. This is known as the Galloway rowing position. The boatman, facing downstream while rowing backwards (pulling), is able to slowly and accurately maneuver the boat around obstacles in the river (backferry).

An interesting point to note is that technically, McKenzie-style driftboats travel downstream stern (back of the boat) first. The oarsman's back is to the bow even though looking at the contemporary boats, the casual observer would believe that they are traveling downstream bow first. This fact has caused controversy between the U.S. Coast Guard and the builders of the boats. If you want to stir the ire of some of the old-time boatmen, just call the pointed end of the McKenzie driftboat the bow. Strangely enough, while developed only one hundred miles or so south, and in spite of frequent interaction between each region's rivermen, the Rogue River style driftboats travel downstream bow (pointed front or bow) first. This subject has been at the root of several controversies between rival guides and boat builders on both rivers. There is some additional discussion and more detail in Chapter Four: The Contemporary Driftboat.

Another subject of controversy is the use of the word "dory." When describing the boat, there are those who prefer to call the driftboat a river dory and there are those who vigorously dispute even the mention of the word dory in the same breath as driftboat. The word itself is an American word taken from an Indian language of Central America's Mosquito Coast. Originally the name of a primitive dugout, the contemporary use is to name a deep, flat-bottomed rowboat with a sharp prow and narrow stern.

As reported in the December 14, 1975 issue of the *Eugene Register-Guard*, Joe Kaarhus, son of one of the principal designers of the driftboat, said that there is only some superficial resemblance between a driftboat and a dory. "The main difference is that the riverboat has a wide bottom and the dory has a deliberately narrow bottom so that when its loaded it'll ride deep and have good sea keeping qualities in the ocean and won't get blown around. The river boat at sea would be at the mercy of the wind—it would get blown around like a piece of thistledown. The dory when loaded or even with men in it will have an appreciable draft. The river boat on the other hand, is made so that as one of my Dad's friends used to say, 'It would float on dew'."

Winter steelheading on the Kilchis River. What the driftboat is really all about.

Roger Fletcher is a man who has spent quite an amount of time devoted to the study of the driftboat and its origins. He built the historical reproductions of the models pictured in this book. His painstaking manner of building his iterations is very faithful to the original lines and details of the full-sized originals. His efforts and acquired knowledge contributed a lot to the historical accuracy of this book. His studies and research have led him to the conclusion that from an academic point of view, the lines of the driftboat clearly suggest that it is a dory boat. Furthermore, he notes that Tom Kaarhus, the man most responsible for the design of the original McKenzie River driftboat, spent a few years in Alaska working in the fishing industry prior to landing in Oregon. In Alaska he was undoubtedly introduced to

the dory-type fishing boats used there during that period in time. Whether or not he was influenced much by those sea-going dories is open to speculation. His son Joe did not believe that to be true.

Roger Fletcher also made the following interesting observation about this controversy: Those who use the boats strictly for river running often refer to it as a dory or a river dory. Those using the boat for fishing almost always call it a driftboat.

Whatever point of view you have or develop, I hope you take the time to open mindedly remember that this is a fishing boat designed for good times. To many of us, the fun continues even off the water when we have the time to, in abject good humor, discuss the controversies of the driftboat. Let us enjoy the argument without ill will simply for the sake of the argument because regardless of the actual truth, it is only academic.

As mainstays of professional fishing guides, driftboats make wonderful fishing platforms. Feisty trout, fierce-fighting aerobic steelhead, and the magnificent chinook salmon have long been favorite targets of driftboating fishermen. Driftboat use has grown from just a few streams in Oregon to streams and rivers throughout the West in a very short time. Today (1999) they are seen coast to coast in both the United States and Canada and are exported for use around the world. Driftboats are even manufactured in foreign countries.

While it is traditional for driftboats to be rowed, it is not unusual to see boatmen using motors when working flat water. This saves their arms and backs, especially when pulling plugs for steelhead or salmon all day long. Motors are quite useful against strong currents and upriver winds as well as to motor along to some favorite holding water. Tidewater sections of our Northwest coastal streams and bigger bodies of water such as the Columbia and Willamette rivers see their share of motored driftboats.

Using a motor sure beats fighting your way back upstream with oars.

Driftboaters use their motors to hold their place amongst other motor boats in the deep and fast water of the Willamette during spring chinook fishing, May 1999.

When in my driftboat, I am usually out for the fishing. Sometimes I am seeking a solitary immersion in the tranquility and excitement of the river. At other times I am exercising, rowing for the sheer joy of being part of the river, the boating, the beauty of it all. There is a peacefulness to being on a river that relaxes your soul.

Practice and experience will continue to add to your enjoyment of the river. Educating yourself to the ways of the river and boating will build your confidence and help you come home safely.

When I first became involved in driftboating it was through the auspices of my friend, Ron Gifford. My first trip in a driftboat was with him on the lower Clackamas River. Ron had just barely begun boating, but luckily the lower Clackamas is not the worst piece of water on which to learn. This first trip was enough, it got me hooked. I had to have a driftboat.

A few months later I acquired my own boat. I spent so much time on the river that it did not take long for me to catch up to Ron in experience. Still, Ron and I

Diagram of the Hindman-style McKenzie River driftboat in skeleton form.

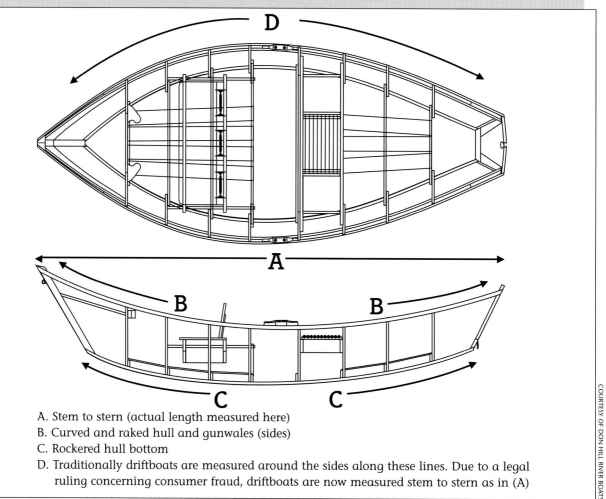

A. Stem to stern (actual length measured here)
B. Curved and raked hull and gunwales (sides)
C. Rockered hull bottom
D. Traditionally driftboats are measured around the sides along these lines. Due to a legal ruling concerning consumer fraud, driftboats are now measured stem to stern as in (A)

Dan Alsup and his father, 'Wild' Bill Alsup, on the last trip of the beer boat before it was painted.

were so green that we figured to use our spare oars the same way that Glen Wooldridge used pike poles on his first trip down the Rogue River—to ward off the rocks and cliff walls. Like Glen, we discovered that using oars to push away from obstacles did not work very well. Those initial trips on Class I and II waters were truly adventures and every bit of whitewater was a treat.

I had no books, videos, or tapes specific to driftboats to help me find my way. Instead, I attended the school of hard rocks on the lower ends of the Clackamas and Sandy rivers. There I gradually learned. If I rowed backwards—if I would pull instead of push on the oars—two good things would happen: I could put on the brakes and slow my downstream momentum and I could pull around or away from where I did not want to be. Thus I could avoid obstacles with which I did not want to connect. This all meant that now I could negotiate whitewater and effectively employ the various fishing techniques that give the driftboater an advantage.

Eventually, I found some books which proved very useful. *Steelhead Drift Fishing* by Bill Luch and *Guide to Floating Whitewater Rivers* by R. W. Miskimins, while not specifically about driftboating, confirmed what I had been learning on my own and filled in a lot of the blanks. They were also a boost to my understanding of the river and its features. I hope this book does that and more for the novice boater who makes use of this book.

The purpose of this book is to give the reader an opportunity to get to know the driftboat, its historical background, and to make the beginner's start a little less tentative. My hope is that even the expert oarsman will find this book useful and worthy of inclusion in his or her library.

This book will not turn a novice into an instant driftboat expert. It can serve as a road map to help get you started in the right direction. A kick in the butt to get you to take some time studying and practicing is not included—the person who seriously wants to increase his skills and acumen must furnish that. The more you put into the sport, the more you learn about it, the more you will get out of it and the better boatman you will be. I sincerely desire to see you on the river safely enjoying the adventures you can find only there. I hope this book is a help towards that end.

Safe and happy boating adventures to you.

—Dan Alsup

Adrenaline-pumped expressions at the top of Martin's Creek Rapid on the McKenzie.

CHAPTER 1

The Early Days

IN THE 1800S, DURING THE EXPLORATION AND charting of the western lands and rivers on the North American continent, rivers were used extensively as highways. Men like Captains Lewis and Clark, William H. Ashley, John C. Fremont and Kit Carson, John Wesley Powell and others, made use of the rivers they charted as they worked to open the frontier to settlement and development. During that exciting period in our history, river travel in the western lands was difficult and dangerous, but it was generally faster and much more practical than going overland.

Pioneer rivermen used everything from Indian-crafted hide boats, birch bark canoes, and crude dugouts, to heavy, keeled, wooden-plank boats. Fremont and Carson even tried a rubber boat imported from Europe during Fremont's first western adventure in 1842. These early craft were occasionally assisted by wind power and often pushed along with long pike poles, but more often they were paddled or rowed. The early frontier boats were usually rowed downstream bow first by oarsmen who faced upstream and were dependent upon pilots who manned sweep oars or rudders to steer their boats around obstacles.

The rapids of our wild Western rivers were both terrorizing and exhilarating to the souls of the early explorers and frontiersmen. Of course many of them, like many of us today, loved adventure and thrived on the adrenaline rush found running big and/or technical water. Water we might consider to be moderate and 'fun' was often immensely difficult and life threatening to the explorers. Many of the rapids we run today with glee were considered impassable by the explorers who had to portage and line their way around them. Lugging heavy provisions, gear, and scientific specimens for hundreds of yards along rocky riverbanks was no picnic. Minor injuries, bruised shins and twisted ankles, added to the misery. The strain of portaging was harder on most of the men than actually running the rapids.

Life preservers (PFDs) were available and used by many on planned river expeditions. Powell and his men could credit their lives to them. Unfortunately, life jackets did not receive high priority on equipment requisitions for overland exploration expeditions, as a result PFDs were in short supply on the frontier. On the Lewis and Clark expedition, a standard rule was followed for safety: Men who couldn't swim walked around the worst rapids. Then as today, a man overboard without a life preserver, was a person with his life in jeopardy, even more so if he cannot swim.

Whirlpools, eddys, quicksand, rocks, rapids, big waves, treacherous currents and undertows contributed to making river journeys into very hazardous adventures. Loss of life associated with river travel was not uncommon. Lapses in judgment and concentration, or just bad luck, were all it took then, and all it takes now for the torrent to claim another life. Amazingly, in spite of poor equipment, inexperience with rivers, simple miscalculations and so forth which resulted in capsized boats and unplanned swims, neither the Lewis and Clark nor the J.W. Powell expedition lost a single life due to drowning or hypothermia.

The heavy boats of the frontier, not known for maneuverability, were at the mercy of the rocks and

Lewis and Clark. As leaders of the corps of discovery, these two men managed to travel thousands of miles without accidental loss of life. Common sense and skills sharpened on the relatively easy waters of the Midwest, and a lot of good luck, brought these men safely home from their adventure.

COURTESY OF INDEPENDENCE NATIONAL HISTORICAL PARK

currents. Their wooden planking was frequently smashed up against midstream boulders during the many unavoidable collisions. Extensive repairs were as common as the rapids. If a boat was to get out of shape and go sideways on or between boulders, more than likely it would breakup. If it did not sink, the damage

Roger Fletcher's model of today's McKenzie River driftboat.

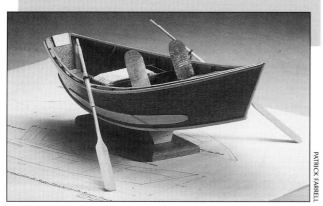

could easily be so severe that repairs were not possible. The damaged or destroyed boats would be either cannibalized for parts or just abandoned. We are very fortunate that we no longer have to depend on those heavy planked boats.

In many ways, modern techniques, design, and materials in use today have made our lives easier and less dangerous. So to, our river adventures in rowed boats are much less arduous and a whale of a lot safer for us than for our exploring forbearers. We play in the same rapids that terrorized frontiersmen. They have been tamed by dynamite, craft of superior design and materials, and the experiences of those pioneering boatmen who went before us—men like John Wesley Powell, Nathan Galloway, Glen Wooldridge, Charlie Foster, Ruell Hawkins, Carey Thompson and his sons, Roy and John West, Veltie Pruitt, Prince Helfrich, Tom Kaarhus, Woodie Hindman, Everett Spaulding and, many, many others just as deserving, but too numerous to mention. Their life's work and play left us a rich legacy of doors opened to the wonders and the beauty of our wild wilderness rivers.

In the early 1890s, Nathaniel 'Than' Galloway, a trapper and hunter based in Vernal, Utah, began using and building small boats. One of the last mountain men, Galloway ran a trap line along the Green River and had discovered that a boat really helped him be more efficient in his work. Spending a lot of time working on the river as he did, Galloway learned much about running white water. He discovered and refined many of the concepts of river-running carried forward today. Instead of the heavy oak boats that Powell used, Galloway's were light and much more maneuverable.

They were flat bottomed to reduce draft so they would float over the shallow waters he encountered. He also has been credited with originating the basic rowing technique which we employ to maneuver our driftboats.

As Than Galloway worked alone, he did not have the luxury of a pilot or oarsman to man the sweep oar or rudder as he rowed, blindly, into the downstream maelstrom. His remedy, either by design or happenstance, was to point the stern downstream and back row to ferry himself into position for a drop or to maneuver around obstacles. Galloway's rowing position was made famous by his 1909 descent of the Green and Colorado rivers through the Grand Canyon guiding Julius Stone's party. It is not inconceivable that accounts of the trip reached the early Rogue and McKenzie boatmen who may have copied his rowing position. On the other hand, it is also reasonable to believe that the rowers on the Oregon rivers discovered the position by trial and error. I figured out how to put on the brakes and backferry without assistance, but

Roger Fletcher's model of Bob Pritchett's Rogue River Special.

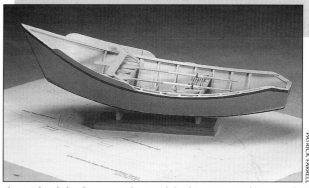

then I had the luxury of a modified McKenzie boat with a stern that looks like a bow. Naturally, I aimed it where I wanted to go, so I started out facing the 'stern'.

Whether Nathaniel Galloway is the single pioneer of this rowing method, or one of a number of rivermen who discovered its advantages around the same time, he is credited with the inception of the idea and is honored today by this standard whitewater rowing position/method bearing his name.

Over the next quarter of a century, rivermen gained experience and background knowledge that led to the metamorphosis of the modern or 'contemporary' driftboat. During this period the old style of heavy planked boats began to give way to lighter more maneuverable boats. Two distinct styles began to emerge, each named for the respective river districts from whence they came—the Rogue and McKenzie. Today the two styles have become so much alike that only the discerning and knowledgeable eye will tell them apart.

CHAPTER 2

Boats of the Rogue River

THE ROGUE RIVER ORIGINATES NEAR CRATER LAKE in the high Cascade Mountains of southern Oregon. For the first fifty miles or so the Rogue River system consists of three tributaries that then join to create the main river. They continue to flow together for another 115 miles or so, through the heart of the rugged Siskiyou Mountains to the river's confluence with the Pacific Ocean at Gold Beach. The Rogue gained its name from a group of French trappers who had trouble with the Indians of the area whom they referred to as The Rogues. The canyons of the Rogue were first settled by miners lured by the prospect of getting rich in the gold fields. Logging and ranching and other agricultural pursuits gradually replaced mining as mainstays of the local economy.

Roger Fletcher's model of Zane Grey boat located at Winkle Bar on the Rogue River.

PATRICK FARRELL

Both logging and mining required heavy loads of supplies, men, and equipment. In spite of its horrific rapids and falls, the Rogue was just too convenient not to be used as a highway. This highway called for boats that were maneuverable and could stand up to the beating this river would give them. The boats would also have to handle a considerable load and be of a design to handle heavy water without swamping. To meet this need, boats were brought or copied from a design that had their origins in the Penebscot River region of Maine. These boats, known as 'log-driving bateaux,' had proved their worth by hauling people and supplies upstream and herding unruly rafts of logs downstream to the mills.

The log-driving bateaux were large, 18 to 36 feet long. They were heavy plank boats rowed by as many

During the later 1800s, log-driving bateaux (boats) from the Penobscot River of Maine were used in the Northwest to haul men, equipment, and supplies upstream to the logging camps. This boat was photographed on the Clearwater River in Idaho.

THE FOREST HISTORY SOCIETY, DURBAN, NC

as six oarsmen. A good crew of oarsmen and pikers could move these boats upstream against some pretty strong currents. Most of the boats of this type used on the Rogue were smaller 18 to 23 feet. When used for trips downstream from Grants Pass to the miners on the most remote and wild sections of the river, these boats were frequently built to be one-way boats. Once the destination was reached, the heavy mining equipment and supplies would be off loaded and the boats either abandoned or dismantled for their lumber.

Here a log-driving bateau hooks up with a raft floating down a Northwest river. The boat appears to have at least three oarsmen and several more crew members. Some boats were so big that six oarsmen were required.

THE FOREST HISTORY SOCIETY, DURBAN, NC

Sailed river-driving bateau. This one carried mail between Gold Beach and Agnes, Oregon on the Rogue River. Note that the lines are identical to the Zane Grey river-driving bateau on this page. Note also, the riverman is using a pike pole to help the boat over the shallows.

COURTESY OF ED KAMMER ROGUE RIVER MAILBOATS

By the turn of the century (1900) a thriving commercial fishery had sprung up. Buyers and processing plants were located at both Gold Beach and at Grants Pass. A resulting commercial infrastructure naturally grew up to supply the needs of the fishermen. As required by need, new equipment and skills were developed as well. The gillnet fishermen had adapted a smaller version of the log-driving bateau to serve as a fishing boat.

This river-driving bateau was about 18 feet with two sets of oarlocks, pointed bow and stern, flat-bottomed with low, flared sides. They were still fairly heavy, being made of straight tight grained wood planks often white Port Orford cedar, yellow or sugar pine, even redwood

and spruce. This type of construction is known as lap strake or board and bat, each board or plank is called a strake. The bottom of this boat was almost flat—not much rocker, this enabled the river 'dory' of the fishermen to float high, displacing enough water to allow the boats to handle a heavier load and still negotiate the shallows associated with the rapids. When traveling downstream, the oars could be manned by one man

Zane Grey's boat, a river-driving bateau. When taken downstream on the Rogue, these early boats were considered one-way boats. When they reached the downriver destination with supplies and mining equipment, they were salvaged for lumber or just abandoned. This boat is a scaled-down version of the log-driving bateau brought to Oregon from Maine. Claude Bardon probably built this boat in the early 1920s.

JOYCE & MARTY SHERMAN

with another using the pike poles to ward off the cliffs and rocks. (Pike poles were about 8 to 10 feet long with sharp steel ends for gripping the bottom and were about as big around as an oar shaft.) Upstream travel required the boatmen pushing with pike poles over the shallows and two men rowing through the deeper sections of water. In the lower river a strong on-shore afternoon

Veltie Pruitt and his good friend and client, Merwin 'Pat' Irish on the Deschutes in this 1938 photo.

COURTESY OF ROY PRUITT

Veltie Pruitt and Merwin 'Pat' Irish on the Crooked River in this 1938 photo.

COURTESY OF ROY PRUITT

breeze made possible the use of sails for upstream travel, and a good downstream wind in the mornings allowed river travel that required much less effort.

This boat is equipped with a spray shield to minimize splash on the paying customers. Early guide and riverman Charlie Foster is at the oars. While there are significant differences between the Rogue and McKenzie-style driftboat, you will have to look closely to find them.

COURTESY OF STEVE PRITCHETT

During this period—the 1880s through the mid to late 1920s—most of the fishermen built their own boats. Although the design was basically the same from one fisherman to another, they all experimented a little with minor modifications. In the mid-1920s, a gillnetter named Glen Wooldridge began building boats for other fishermen working the Rogue around Grants Pass. He was constantly experimenting. Glen built boats of sugar pine and spruce in addition to the

standard cedar. He rarely built more than two to four boats of exactly the same design and materials. Gradually a distinct style of driftboat emerged.

About that same time Glen began guiding 'dudes' on fishing expeditions. This necessitated a boat designed for anglers instead of gillnetters. His 'Rogue River Specials' were designed to float down the river and then be rowed and poled (later motored) back upstream either to the take out or to get another float down the drift. These boats were about 20 to 23 feet long and still resembled the river-driving bateaux, but changes were taking place. The flat bottom was curved up in the bow a little to allow easier turning. Extra strakes were added in the front third of the boat to give the passengers a drier ride through big waves.

On Rogue-style boats, the pointed end has always been the bow and it has always traveled downstream bow-first. Notice that the bottom of the boat has a large flat area as opposed to the McKenzie's continuous rocker. The top of the stern is also canted to allow for an outboard motor to be mounted. This particular boat is the last boat built by Bob Pritchett.

COURTESY OF STEVE PRITCHETT

Eventually the stern was squared off. This allowed for the use of motors. By the late 1930s, Glen had begun using plywood to build the hulls of his boats. He had been encouraged to try it by a Portland-area lumberman. Almost immediately plywood became the boatbuilder's material of choice and the planked boats of the Rogue River began to fade into history.

In 1951, Wooldridge sold his guiding business to Bob Pritchett. Glen and his sons concentrated on building driftboats as well as perfecting the jet sled (a motored boat). Pritchett continued to refine the Rogue River driftboat design until its look was distinguishable from the McKenzie River boats only to the discerning eye of a riverman familiar with the differences between the two.

Ray Heater and Cyrus Happy have continued to build boats that follow the lines of the original square-ended (Rapid Robert) driftboats. They also continue to produce the Rogue River-style boat like Bob Pritchett's boat pictured on the previous page. It follows the Rogue-style design that includes more flair on the sides (three to five degrees) than the McKenzie boats and a dead flat section on the bottom that is different from the McKenzie's full rocker bottom. This flat section allows the boat to draw less water and therefore to float a little higher than its northern counterpart. This is important on the Rogue because the river trips usually last several days. The boats have to carry two fishermen, a guide, and all the food, clothing, and camping gear needed on a trip that could last up to five days.

Glen Wooldridge and son Bruce, bringing a boat and a dude (a paying customer) over Kelsey Falls on the wild-and-scenic stretch of the Rogue River. Note the use of two sets of oarlocks and oars. Although the boat has been built up in the bow with an extra plank or 'strake' to minimize splash on the 'dude', this boat does have strong similarities to the Zane Grey boat pictured on page 15.

COURTESY OF FLORENCE ARMAN

In the auditorium above the old Eugene City Hall, Veltie Pruitt built his first plywood driftboat. (circa 1939)

COURTESY OF ROY PRUITT

CHAPTER 3

Boats of the McKenzie River

THE MCKENZIE RIVER HEADS IN CLEAR LAKE HIGH IN Oregon's Cascade Mountains. It flows nearly ninety miles to its confluence with the Willamette River just north of Eugene. Unlike the Rogue, the McKenzie River did not have a commercial fishery, but it did have a highway that ran its length. It was very accessible early on to fishermen and tourists. In 1909 Carey Thompson conducted a guided float trip (the first) down the river with a tourist. Within a few years, the guiding business became a strong draw to a growing tourist industry along the river, an industry that expanded to include lodges, stores, restaurants, boat builders, and shuttle drivers.

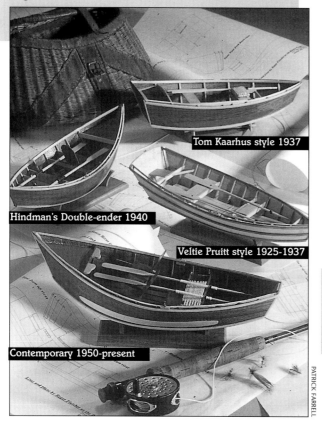

Roger Fletcher models of the McKenzie River driftboats.

Tom Kaarhus style 1937

Hindman's Double-ender 1940

Veltie Pruitt style 1925-1937

Contemporary 1950-present

PATRICK FARRELL

Their boats were old-fashioned rowboats or skiffs. These rough homemade boats did not look like the boats of the Rogue, but in some ways they were similar: Usually made with cedar, the planked boats had flat

Early McKenzie guides—Carey Thompson's sons, York and Milo—fishing from an old rowboat in the late teens or early twenties. This was the kind of boat used before the West brothers started changing the design.

THOMPSON

bottoms and low sides. Like the early Rogue boats, they were heavy enough to withstand banging and grinding on the rocks and gravely shallows. These old skiffs, sometimes called 'old scows', were long (anywhere from eighteen to twenty-two feet) and narrow. And they were just as difficult to maneuver as they were to row. The low sides let so much water splash onboard that regular bailing was an ongoing task. The ability to build light, tough and maneuverable craft was still years in the future, but the know-how was being discovered bit by bit by the early boatmen.

Form Followed Function

Like their contemporaries on the Rogue, the early boatmen on the McKenzie built most of their own boats. They were basically the same style, but everyone had

Veltie Pruitt's old scow. His first boat and Dallas Murphy, first person he guided, friend 'Rick' Richardson at the oars. Boat is typical of the old skiff-type rowed boats that predated the wider, deeper, and lighter driftboats.

COURTESY OF ROY PRUITT

Hall of Fame guide Kenny King at the oars in a board-and-batten boat that predates Veltie Pruitt's little driftboat. Kenny says this boat leaked like crazy until it had been in the river for a while, then it would swell up and a little tar in the cracks would keep out most of the river.

an idea; the best ones were copied and the ones that didn't work were left behind. In about 1920 or so, a couple of brothers tried some new ideas.

According to John West, he and his brother, Roy, built a boat with major changes. Their boat was fourteen feet long and four feet wide. They figured that if it was shorter and wider than the usual boats it would be stable and wouldn't tip so much. Rivermen laughed at its shape. "Milo Thompson said it looked like a bathtub." This great-grandfather of present-day driftboats was unusual to look at, but its improved design allowed it to float over shallows that grounded older-style boats. Why drag and push a boat over gravel bars when you can float it over? The Thompson brothers stopped laughing after they saw how well it worked. Milo Thompson tried it out and liked it so well that he borrowed it every chance he got after that. Then, as other boatmen built new boats, the West's improvements were adopted. ("The Boat the McKenzie River

Roger Fletcher's model of the Veltie Pruitt boat.

Spawned"; by Jim Boyd; *Eugene Register-Guard*; December 14, 1975.)

Along about 1925-26, a Eugene-area minister turned guide, Veltie Pruitt, consulted with a Norwegian immigrant named Torkel 'Tom' Kaarhus to build a boat similar in design to the Wests' boats. The boat Veltie built is probably the closest thing to a grandfather of the driftboats of the 1990s. He got Kaarhus, who was a shopman at the Ford-Nelson Planning Mill and experienced at building various kinds of boats, to mill his lumber (lightweight spruce instead of cedar) to full-dimension 1 x 12s thirteen feet long. The bottom of this boat was made of three planks that made it three feet wide. Veltie's boat was a small square-sterned improvement on the Wests' design. It had a flat bottom that was slightly upswept in both bow and stern. This meant that by using a backferry rowing method, this very lightweight boat could be maneuvered much more easily through technical water than could the older styles of boats.

Veltie Pruitt fishing from the first 'light' McKenzie River driftboat.

In about 1926 or '27, Veltie and his good friend and fishing companion Dr. Rebhan, were on an excursion in the new style McKenzie boat when a fellow on the bank beckoned them to pull in. Curious to see who it was, Veltie rowed over to the bank. Prince Helfrich, a young guide, had been watching them maneuver the little boat with unabashed admiration. "Where did you get that boat," he queried. "It sure looks like a dandy." A short time later Prince Helfrich was trying out Veltie Pruitt's little boat. Prince liked the boat so much that he asked Veltie to build him one. Veltie agreed and a lifelong friendship was born.

The new friendship was to lead the pair of pioneer rivermen on many happy boating adventures. Veltie and Prince made the first descents of several rivers including the middle Deschutes and the John Day. They made a couple of trips down the upper Rogue

This series of pictures was taken at the time Veltie Pruitt and his adventuring cohort, Prince Helfrich, made the first descent of the upper Rogue River. They started their river adventure below the dam at Prospect. In order to launch their boats, those determined boatmen made use of the tramway that had been installed to help construct the dam. In this first picture at the top of the tramway, Prince and his wife, Marjorie, with the first little lightweight driftboat built by Veltie, Veltie's 1929 Model 'A' Ford, and his trailer made from a Model 'T' axel.

COURTESY OF ROY PRUITT

After loading a boat onto the tram, these fearless thrill-seekers posed for a picture because they knew that some-day would be placed in this book to record for posterity.

COURTESY OF ROY PRUITT

One boat down and Prince's wife, Marjorie, lends her pretty face to the moment.

COURTESY OF ROY PRUITT

Prince Helfrich negotiating the rock garden below the powerhouse at Prospect on the first descent of that section of the Rogue River in this 1931 photo.

COURTESY OF ROY PRUITT

Once down, Veltie and Prince begin the first descent of the Upper Rogue River in a driftboat.

COURTESY OF ROY PRUITT

Fletcher model of the original McKenzie River driftboat: aka the Rapid Robert; aka square-ender.

PATRICK FARRELL

which got the attention of the boatmen on that southern river, including Glen Wooldridge, and undoubtedly influenced to some degree or another the evolution of that region's boats. The McKenzie River driftboat had made its presence known, it had been born, now all it had to do was grow up.

The McKenzie River Driftboat

In 1935, Torkel "Tom" G. Kaarhus, the native son of Norway who had helped Veltie Pruitt with his little boat, leased an old building next door to Williams Bakery in Eugene, Oregon. Moving his family into the apartment upstairs, Kaarhus opened a crafts shop downstairs. In his shop, Tom was able to draw upon his childhood pleasures and pastimes: skiing and boating. (He was born and lived on a Norwegian island). In the winter he skied and in summer he boated and fished. It was only natural for him to build skis and boats.

Torkel (Tom) G. Kaarhus: master craftsman and designer/builder of the original McKenzie River driftboat.

COURTESY OF MAURYA KAARHUS

Tom Kaarhus was not only a master woodcrafter, he was a musician, scholar, boater, and fisherman. His love of music led him to singing and directing in both the Lutheran Church he attended and the Norsemen, a men's chorus that represented the sons of Norway. His love of fishing and boating led Kaarhus to building all kinds of boats. He built motorboats, sailboats, and even an ocean-going trimaran that sailed the Pacific. It was only natural that he would build boats to be used on the shallow fast rivers in the vicinity of Eugene. Eventually Tom Kaarhus gained quite a reputation for the work he did perfecting the design and for building many of the original McKenzie River driftboats.

McKenzie guides, Carl Baker and Howard Montgomery, enjoying the float during an early whitewater parade on the McKenzie River. They are in an original Kaarhus-style McKenzie River driftboat (aka square-ender, aka Rapid Robert). This boat was built using board-and-batten type construction.

COURTESY OF MAURYA KAARHUS

Tom's first riverboats were similar to boats currently in use in the area. They were plank boats of board and batten construction. The planks were made from various local woods including fir, cedar, and spruce milled down to 3/8 of an inch thick and up to a full foot wide. Richard Helfrich was quoted in *Wooden Boat Magazine*, issue No. 52 by John Babbs, as saying that those old plank boats "leaked to beat the band. They also took water over the top and after we'd fish for a while we'd bail for a while." Tom Kaarhus made some serious improvements to the riverboat that both refined the design and defined the McKenzie River driftboat.

Beginning with the successful boat design that he and Veltie Pruitt had collaborated on, Kaarhus fashioned the sides higher and added some flaring to give the occupants a drier ride. Rocker (the curvature of the bottom) was increased to make for quicker turning, thereby increasing maneuverability. He also installed a rope seat that went a long way towards keeping the boatman's spirits up and his backside dry. Tom also increased the height and rounded off the transom in order to keep the dudes drier in the big waves.

In 1937 Tom Kaarhus built what was probably the first plywood driftboat. The strength of the driftboat was increased and its weight decreased. That was the beginning of the end for planked boats on the McKenzie. This square-ended boat with its high tombstone-shaped transom is considered by most to be the original McKenzie River driftboat. Yet, the metamorphosis of the driftboat was not complete.

Tom Kaarhus' Craft Shop that sat next door to the Williams Bakery until they needed room for a parking lot. This picture was found hanging in the Izzy's Pizza Parlor on Franklin Blvd., not far from its origin. The men in the photo are some of Tom's craftsmen employees.

COURTESY OF LANE COUNTY MUSEUM

In the 1950s, Tom's son, Joseph, joined him and together they continued to build and refine the design of the driftboats. Just as other boat builders before them, Tom and Joe also utilized and improved upon the innovations of others. As long as the business remained, their reputation for fine quality boats grew. Tom continued to build boats until he was incapacitated by illness in the early 1960s and death in 1962. Joseph built boats for several years until shortly after the lease on the original site of the shop expired and economics eventually led to the demise of the business.

Kenny King with a Kaarhus boat in about 1940 on a homemade trailer. It has Model 'T' axle and wheels, and springs from a buggy seat on a 2x4 frame.

COURTESY OF KENNEY KING

Tom's wife, Adena Kaarhus, and friends fishing the Siuslaw River in a plywood Rapid Robert about 1949.

COURTESY OF MAURYA KAARHUS

Early McKenzie driftboats were rowed with both the boatman and the stern facing downstream. When big waves were encountered, the oarsman would have to 'turn a corner' or angle the squared stern into the wave to help break through it. Otherwise the boat could lose its forward momentum (stall out) and even slide back down the wave. This could be disastrous if the upstream bow became buried in the wave behind or even if the boatman just lost shape (got turned sideways in a trough between waves) and couldn't recover. When slow water was encountered and the boatman wanted to make time, they would 'bow down,' that is, turn the bow downstream so he could pull on the oars to row with power.

Joe Kaarhus-built boat on the Sandy River in spring of 1999.

Not long after Tom Kaarhus began building boats, a young Texan immigrant, Woodie Hindman, came into town. When he wasn't fishing, boating or, guiding, Hindman operated a small hotel, The Hampton on 7th street. In his heart, Woodie was not satisfied. He wanted to do something that would keep him more in touch with the outdoors he loved so much. Being a part-time guide and an avid fisherman and boatman, learning how to build driftboats was a natural progression. He made a deal with Tom Kaarhus. If Tom would teach him how to build boats, Woodie would work for Kaarhus for a while without pay. The arrangement

Woodie Hindman rowing major whitewater on the Middle Fork.

COURTESY OF DAVE HELFRICH

worked well and after a time Woodie was ready to strike out on his own. Woodie started building boats in the basement of his hotel and did well. His boat business grew. In 1941 when he reached the point where he needed more space than his basement afforded, Woodie opened a shop across the Willamette River from Eugene, at 1607 Main Street in Springfield.

Tom's son, Joe, and one of his driftboats at a Eugene boat show in the late 50s.

COURTESY OF MAURYA KAARHUS

Woodie Hindman was never the craftsman that Kaarhus was, but he did build good boats. He was known more for his improvements to the boat. Things like seats that slid on pipes and numerous other little improvements including some very important design changes that are discussed in full in the next chapter. Many of his friends thought him to be a great improviser, someone who would have done well for a big company as an inventor who just thought up new ideas. John West saw him as a keen observer who could adapt clever ideas that he saw. He noted that Hindman

spent a lot of time observing the boats of other builders. Woodie was also popular with the guides, being one himself.

His shop saw all of the guides of the region. They would stop by to see what was new, to put in orders and buy new boats. Often they would request modifications. Glen Wooldridge, of Rogue River fame, would always pay a visit when in town. Some say it was out of professional courtesy, others say it was to look for ideas that he could incorporate into his own boats. (Rumor has it that the two were more rivals than friends). A lot of the guys would just come by to visit and talk 'shop'.

Woodie was a highly respected driftboat builder in the McKenzie River region for about 20 years or so until he sold out to Marty Rathje. During Woodie's career, the driftboat completed its metamorphosis and emerged the contemporary driftboat that we know today. Woodie Hindman passed on in 1976 when on vacation in Parker, Arizona. He suffered a heart attack while cleaning fish on the banks of the river. Rathje who purchased Woodie's business continued to refine the quality of workmanship until his own retirement.

Weathered, old Woodie Hindman-built square-ender's final resting place. It still sports the original brass plate bearing the Hindman's name.

COURTESY OF DAVID RODRIGUEZ, RICK ALSUP PHOTO

CHAPTER 4

The Contemporary Driftboat

The Metamorphosis

For several years Woodie built the Kaarhus-style square-ender or Rapid Robert boat. During this period of time he became acquainted with other noted boatmen. A natural exchange of ideas took place, with each borrowing or adopting innovations from another. When Glen Wooldridge was in town, he would stop by Woodie's shop. While there is no direct evidence that the two boatmen actually collaborated with one another, there can be no doubt that they had some influence on each other and each other's boats, subtly borrowing or improving on one another's design. Today we might call that interaction 'corporate espionage' even though there was nothing covert about it.

Roger Fletcher model of Woodie's double-ender.

PATRICK FARRELL

waves, rather than try to spin the boat around in heavy water he simply sat on the bale of hay that he was carrying for a friend who lived downstream a ways and rowed with the pointed bow facing downstream. Hindman discovered that he liked the way his pointed

Woodie Hindman: The man, the boat, and breakfast.

COURTESY OF KENNY KING

Everett Spaulding (left) and Woodie Hindman. It was Spaulding's request for a small transom in the bow for a motor mount that led Woodie to engineer the contemporary or modified McKenzie River driftboat.

COURTESY OF KENNY KING

Woodie was quite a fisherman and an oarsman in his own right. He was known for the trips he made down the Rogue, the Deschutes, and other Northwest rivers that offered good fishing and challenging whitewater. In about 1943 he took a trip on the Salmon River in Idaho. While rowing his square-ender, Hindman got turned around backwards in some pretty fair-sized

Woodie Hindman and his friend Kenny Taylor in double-enders coming through a rock garden known as Haystack Rocks on the Middle Fork.

COURTESY OF KENNY KING

bow cut through the waves. He did not have to turn a corner to keep from stalling out as he did with the square-ended stern. This was something that had been a concern for him for some time. When he got home from Idaho, in an inspired state of mind, Woodie carried the lines of the stern out to a point.

Now the stern of the boat would cut the waves like a bow. Thus the double-ender was reborn. The double-ender idea had existed for a long time and had been used on the Rogue and other places where the log- and river-driving bateau were present. (Refer to photo of Zane Grey's boat on page 15). No doubt Woodie was influenced by the older styles and even the Rogue style currently in use. In any case, Woodie Hindman radically changed the design of the McKenzie River driftboat. His double-ended creation became the new standard until he redefined the boat one more time.

A few years later, in 1946, a fishing guide named Everett Spaulding, asked for a driftboat on which he could mount a motor, so Woodie placed a small transom on the bow to make a place to mount Spaulding's motor. Hindman was not satisfied with the way it looked or worked so he re-engineered his double-ender design to build a new boat for Spaulding. When it was complete it had a different look and feel. Many of the guides liked it and it caught on. Soon this new design

became the standard for the modern driftboat. A few old-timers like Prince Helfrich preferred the original double-ender design, but in spite of their resistance to change, the modification caught on. And the nomenclature of the driftboat changed. Popular thinking has it that the motor is always mounted on the stern. This precipitated an issue that has been a bone of contention ever since.

The Controversy of the Bow and Stern

When Woodie installed the transom he effectively changed the driftboat so that the bow became the stern and vice versa. This change also bridged the gap between the Rogue boats that had always been rowed bow first (pointed end) downstream. When rowing the contemporary boat, the McKenzie oarsman, while still facing downstream, now faces the bow. You can see how this also redefined the Galloway position. Old-timers still bristle when they hear the bow being called the stern and the stern the bow, because you don't anchor from the stern and no one likes Johnnie-come-latelies or outsiders messing around with their traditions.

Keith Steele, a prolific driftboat builder, went round and around with the U.S. Coast Guard over the placement of weight placards and hull identification numbers. The Coast Guard wanted the hull ID on the bow and the weight placard on the stern. The Coast Guard figured by being 'The Government' agency that it is, they did not have to regard the right or will of the people and to hell with tradition, history, or even the facts; the pointed end has to be the bow. It seems that the feds won. Most folks and even some of the boat-builders, call the pointed end the bow. So, with all due respect to those who went before me, the modern or contemporary McKenzie driftboats are considered by the authorities and most boaters to travel downstream bow first.

Over the years there have been continued modifications, refinements, and innovative design changes. Today's builders (2000) still look for ways to improve their boats. New materials have made their mark but the driftboats we see today still look a lot like Woodie Hindman's because his basic design is still followed.

Dan Alsup, while visiting with Don Hill, admires one of Don's beautifully crafted Hindman-style driftboats.

RICK ALSUP

A couple of Veltie Pruitt's clients. Note the fly deck is in the stern of this square-ended McKenzie boat. That is because then, as now, (technically) driftboats are run downstream stern first.

COURTESY OF ROY PRUITT

Wooden boats are still built commercially and there is nothing wrong with a good wooden boat, in fact many professionals prefer wood. Plywood is actually the strongest of the three materials used in driftboats (considering the strength-to-weight ratio) and with a good mat and epoxy coating, wood can be fairly low maintenance but a craftsman is required to build them and handle the maintenance. Another advantage wood boats have is that in contrast to aluminum and fiberglass, wood floats for at least awhile. The price of a fine wood boat is no longer cheaper than aluminum or fiberglass because today good-quality wood is harder to come by and is more expensive. Labor costs have also risen tremendously. The result is most driftboats today are made of aluminum or fiberglass.

These materials make the boats a little more impervious to collisions, groundings, and broaches. This ruggedness, along with a long life-span and low maintenance, is the aspect of aluminum and fiberglass driftboats that make them so highly desirable. Coast Guard rules for most boats made in the United States require

enough floatation to render them unsinkable. This rule does not apply to driftboats. Most are designed to sink if capsized or swamped, (a safety feature to prevent a swimmer from being crushed between the boat and rocks?). However, there are some fiberglass models now being built with enough flotation built-in to make them unsinkable. These boats are designed for extreme whitewater.

Wooden boats do need a little more care and/or maintenance such as sanding and painting, not to mention occasional patching and caulking. However, if just a little care is taken to keep the boat clean and dry and if you are good enough to avoid collisions with most of the normal river obstacles, your maintenance hours will be reduced. A well-made, traditional, wooden driftboat is still a highly prized possession of many boaters. This includes professional guides as well as weekend fishermen. Maintenance of a wooden driftboat is a labor of love to those boatmen who still prefer their handcrafted wood boats. Even today, a lot of the driftboats seen on the McKenzie River are old-fashioned, handcrafted, wooden driftboats.

Aluminum Driftboats

The late 1950s brought on the advent of the aluminum driftboat. Aluminum boats have come a long way since their inception. According to Don Hill, a popular wooden driftboat builder and McKenzie guide, aluminum was first used in a driftboat about 1957 by Clark Metal Works in Eugene. Bob Wooldridge, son of Glen Wooldridge, claims that his father built the first aluminum driftboat about the same time. On the other hand, Willie Illingsworth, founder of Alumaweld and Willie Boats, recalls the first boat being built by an obscure company 'down south' for a Klamath Falls family. It was a strange looking affair being riveted together rather than welded.

Speaking of Willie Illingsworth, no book about driftboats would be complete without the story of Wild Willie Illingsworth. Willie Illingsworth was a Rogue River guide with his own ideas about driftboats. One day when talking to Glen Wooldridge, Illingsworth told Glen that he [Willie] could improve upon the Wooldridge design. Now, old Glen was surely impressed with this youngster telling him his boat wasn't good enough and about how he could improve on his

Before Mt. St. Helens blew its top, the Toutle was prime fishing water. An early aluminum driftboat took these two anglers to these nice steelhead and salmon in the 1970s.

COURTESY OF BILL SCHMAUCH AND LEE HASLET

[Glen's] design. Willie wasn't through just yet either. Next thing you know, Willie was asking Wooldridge to build him one, with his improvements of course—and out of aluminum. Now Glen was known for his ability

to become a little crotchety and he must have been just a little irritated. His reply to Willie was somewhat less than courteous, "I don't have time Willie, why don't you go build your own damn boat!"

Willie Illingsworth tackles Blossom Bar Rapid in a photo from an early Alumaweld brochure.

COURTESY OF WILLIE ILLINGSWORTH

The seed had been planted. Wild Willie was not to be deterred. He wanted his boat. He wanted it with his improvements and an aluminum hull. So in 1971 Willie Illingsworth built his first aluminum driftboat. He tried it out and liked what he had. Soon afterward, Illingsworth founded Alumaweld and began producing aluminum-hulled driftboats. It didn't take long before other fishing guides on the rivers saw that the strength and durability combined with the ease of maintenance made these metal driftboats something to covet.

Because of the popularity of his boat it was not long before Willie had taken so many orders to build his modified McKenzie River boats that he was backed up for a year—figuring one boat per week. With that kind of growth going on, and the potential for even more, a healthy chunk of change is required. Willie took on an out-of-state investment partner in order to gain the capital needed to cover the growth of the company.

As the company grew and prospered, so did Willie's reputation for his fine design. Unfortunately partnerships

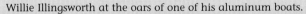

Willie Illingsworth at the oars of one of his aluminum boats.

COURTESY OF WILLIE ILLINGSWORTH/WILLIE BOATS

do not always work well. After about six years in business, Willie was pushed out in a leveraged buyout. To forestall competition from Willie Illingsworth, the master designer, his partners insisted that a standard no-compete clause be included in the buyout agreement which was to remain in force for four years.

Alumaweld continued building driftboats and branched out to include jet sleds. They were eventually bought out by Stevens Marine and continue to enjoy an excellent reputation for fine boats.

Dan Alsup sneaking around a giant haystack at McIver Park on the Clackamas River.

DONNA ALSUP

During those four years 'Willie's R and D' produced rafting frames, aluminum dry boxes, camp kitchens, and truck racks. Anything Willie could find a need for in order to cover living and boating. When the four years were over, Willie's driftboats were once again available to the rivermen. Willie developed a clipper bow (outward flair in the top third of the bow stem) to keep his passengers drier. He also patented a process in which the side rails around the gunwale are of one-

Sean Blackstone displays this nice Clackamas River hatchery steelhead.

piece extruded construction. This innovation added a lot of strength and stability to the design and cut labor costs big time. Illingsworth has continued to this date to produce his popular modified McKenzie River driftboat while still looking for ways to make it better and maintain his motto, "Willie Boats, Simply the Best."

Fiberglass Boats

During the 1960s, there were several attempts to build fiberglass driftboats. The glass boats were heavy at first and did not compete successfully with wood or aluminum boats. Roy Pruitt had one of if not the very first fiberglass driftboat. He experienced problems with the bottom needing repeated repairs and did not find the tracking to be satisfactory. He believed that the rounded chine allowed too much slippage. Other early problems

Watertight decks make this fiberglass boat harder to swamp in the big waters of rivers like the Colorado of the Grand Canyon.

COURTESY OF RON LAVIGUEURE/LAVRO BOATS

Bruce Belles of Clackamas Marine launching a Clackacraft fiberglass driftboat the hard way, through the woods on the way to the cliff. Clackacraft boats have a reputation across the United States for toughness.

COURTESY OF CLACKAMAS MARINE

had to do with construction methods used and the balsa wood core used on some of the initial boats.

In the early 1970s, Andre Laviguere, of Eastside Boats teamed up with his brother, Ron, who had a background working with fiberglass in the aerospace field at Boeing. They formed a new business, Lavro Boats that set the standard for fiberglass driftboats. With Ron as materials engineer and using Andre's basic wooden boat design, the brothers began to produce a glass boat that was in the same league as wood and aluminum. Their boats rivaled aluminum for strength and durability and at the same time compared with the warmth and quietness of wood.

When you consider its advantages, a well-made fiberglass boat is hard to beat. The boat-builder has the option of varying the thickness of the hull. He can make it thicker, in the chine for example, where extra

Ron Lavigueure with one of his fiberglass creations. No matter how many times I do it or see it done, dragging a driftboat down a steep bank like this makes me cringe. But it doesn't hurt this tough fiberglass boat.

COURTESY OF RON LAVIGUEURE/LAVRO BOATS

strength is needed, and a little less thick in the upper hull area. This adds strength and still holds the weight down to roughly equal that of wood- and aluminum-hulled boats. Fiberglass has yet another advantage—the plastic will dent like aluminum rather than puncture like wood. This kind of fiberglass (hand-laid mat) has quite a bit of flexibility. After receiving a dent, fiberglass will spring back to its original form, where aluminum stretches and is impossible to hammer back into perfect shape. The folks that own fiberglass boats like the fact that the boat stays a little warmer in the winter. Your feet do not freeze to it. In the summer, it stays cool to the touch whereas aluminum fly decks can get so hot that you can fry an egg on them. Both wood and aluminum boats need a resin added to the bottom of the boat to help them slide over the shallow gravels and rocks without sticking. Fiberglass boats slide easily over gravel without extra resin.

A fiberglass boat drifting below the Grand Tetons in Wyoming.

COURTESY CLACKAMAS MARINE

The main disadvantage of fiberglass is in the manufacturing process. Because fiberglass products are hand manufactured, the consumer is strictly at the mercy of the builder's integrity and ability to supervise his artisans. The strength of a fiberglass boat is in the matting not in the resin. The fibers are more than one hundred times stronger than the resin. The secret of a good fiberglass boat is while laying up the mat, squeeze out as much resin between layers as possible. This will leave the finished product tough and resilient.

Today there are many manufacturers, both backyard builders and bigger commercial outfits, who are building aluminum boats. Others are using fiberglass to build outstanding driftboats, proven to be as rugged and maintenance-free as their aluminum counterparts. There are still quite a few wooden driftboats built by aficionados of the warm beauty of a hand-crafted wooden boat. Unfortunately, they are seen less and less except along the McKenzie where wood is a tradition. Although there are many subtle design variations, most modern driftboats of today are recognizable as McKenzie River driftboats.

CHAPTER 5

Purchasing Your First Driftboat

BEFORE LEARNING TO ROW, IT WOULD BEHOOVE you to have your own boat. Most oarsmen have a hard time giving up their oars for long and very few are going to lend you a boat in which to learn. Even if you could borrow a boat, would you really want to come home and tell your good buddy about a new dent or the caved-in hull? Would you like to explain why you left it parked on the bottom of the river? (Especially when he has a Deschutes trip scheduled for the upcoming weekend—with his boss.)

Try explaining this to the buddy from whom you borrowed it. Whitehorse Rapid victim recovered by Mark Angel.

COURTESY MARK ANGEL

Just after the big '96 flood, some friends and I drifted the lower Clackamas River between Carver and Riverside Park. Ron Gifford and Sean Blackstone were in Ron's well-maintained, wooden double-ender. Gordon Phillips and I were in my aluminum boat. Gordon wanted to row. That was fine with me, since I would be able to concentrate on some serious fishing.

Over the previous several months, Gordon had been learning the sticks (to row). He was still a novice oarsman, but he was no slouch. He did a fine job bringing the boat down through the first quarter of a mile or so. He had to negotiate a technical little rifle and then a Class I rapid with some standing waves three feet high. A little past this rapid there were a couple of fresh trees down in the river—a gift of the recent flood. One protruded from the right bank and one from the left. In this case, an experienced oarsman would have had no trouble pulling off the left tree, then turning about 90 degrees and pulling off the downstream tree on the right. Ron, in his double-ender, slipped on through with no problem, but Gordon lacked Ron's experience.

After getting around the first tree just fine, Gordon suffered one of the most common problems faced by rookie oarsmen. In the pinch, he got nervous and became confused. Instead of automatically reacting, he was trying to think his way through. His rowing actions all became backward. He could not spin the boat to face that next tree to save his life. In water heavy enough to produce standing waves, we went into the tree sideways. Before it was over we had nearly capsized, lost an oar while bending a perfectly stout brass oarlock all to hell, gone under the tree and over a log. I ended up on the fly deck, which was good, because the boat was about half to three quarters full of cold, cold, Clackamas ice water. Gordon managed to grab the spare oar (with plenty of loud encouragement from me) and started a backferry. That pulled us over to the bank as I bailed like a madman. We reached the bank and emptied the boat.

When it was over, Gordon was more than happy to relinquish the oars. He didn't row any more that day. I am not sure this hour or so on the sticks was good for Gordon because shortly after this incident he bought himself a jet sled. Ron and Sean, while enjoying the show, had stood by to help us and managed to rescue my errant oar. Gordon and I had had enough adventure for one day. Now that it's over and some years have gone by, Gordon remembers it as a "great adventure and a good time." We had all learned first-hand how fast things could go awry.

You understand now, why it is easier on your friends to own your own boat. Better to jeopardize yours than theirs. Besides, having one available is a must for those spur-of-the-moment runs to the river, when you find yourself with a few extra hours and the fish are running hot. Also, you can see the importance of becoming very intimate with your oars before venturing out on a river.

Choosing your boat is another matter. There are so many builders building so many different models out of the various materials. It seems the guides who are not driving jet sleds are mostly in aluminum boats. All the old-timers swear by their beautiful wooden boats. The fly fishermen in Montana love their fiberglass boats. There must be an easy answer, right? Wrong!

There are two methods for choosing the correct driftboat for you. The best way to choose a driftboat is the scientific method; the other way is the knucklehead method. The scientific method is the way that the cool, careful, sophisticated boatman to be (or the highly experienced professional) would go about choosing a driftboat. The other method is how the rest of us buy driftboats.

The Scientific Method

The first consideration for most of us is financial. How much money should you budget. Of course in that process you will have to decide whether you are looking for a new or used boat. In order to get a realistic idea about prices and value look in several areas. For new boat prices, visit with builders and dealers. Check the newspaper ads for used boats. One good place to look is the bulletin board in your favorite toy store (a.k.a sporting goods shop). By taking the time to research the prices of both new and used boats you will get a good idea of value and rates of depreciation. The more time you spend studying the values, the more potential you will have to negotiate a good deal and avoid being taken advantage of.

Next, define the kind of water in which you intend to boat. Will you be boating in narrow, obstacle filled slow water that you find on the lower ends of the coastal steams? Will you be in light whitewater such as the lower Clackamas or Sandy Rivers? Do you prefer to spend your time on the bigger water of the mighty Deschutes or the wild whitewaters of the scenic wilderness stretches of the Rogue?

Ron Gifford's wooden double-ender.

How about fishing? Will you be: Pulling plugs? fly fishing? drift-fishing? Will you be using a combination of methods or another method?

What about passengers? Are you fishing with friends, business clients, or alone?

Do you boat for fun or for profit? Will most of your excursions be one-day or multi-day trips?

Glen Wooldridge in an early aluminum driftboat.

By answering these questions first, your search for a driftboat will most likely be pleasant and effective.

Having answered these questions your answer could result in the following examples. If you are on a tight budget, and will be taking day trips by yourself or with an occasional friend, on the middle section of the Rogue, you could probably get by with a standard 14- to 16-foot wooden McKenzie boat. On the other hand, if you were going to be pulling plugs on the Kenai River in Alaska, taking along 2 to 4 paying clients on multi-day excursions, a 20-foot aluminum boat would fit the bill. If you are a fly fisherman working the Henry's Fork, you might like one of the low-profile fiberglass boats that present less hull for the wind to catch and come set up with pedestal seats fore and aft.

After you have defined your needs and rivers, take some time to talk to experienced oarsmen and boatbuilders. Most folks will be flattered that you asked, and happy to give you their perspectives on which boat to fit yourself into and how to fit the boat to yourself. You will probably get as many different ideas as people you talk to. Ultimately the decision you make will result from your own conclusion after sorting through all the information you receive. I recommend that you study Chapter Four: "Outfitting Your Boat" so you can know what equipment you need to round out your outfit before you hit the river. This may help you find a bargain or at least know what to ask for when it comes time to making a deal.

I spotted an ad for some used driftboats at a boat retailer. The boats were all aluminum and in my price range so I popped on over to get a peek. As I recall, these boats were in pretty good shape. One of them in particular had everything I needed. It came equipped with a sharp-looking trailer, three old oars, an anchor and rope, and bracket with a pulley and jam cleat. There were heavy brass oarlocks, good seats, and plenty of dry storage. The 16-foot modified McKenzie boat was loaded and ready for the river. Best of all, the price was

Boat-builder Bruce Belles on Idaho's South Fork of the Snake. Fall Creek enters the river in a spectacular way. This is a fine way to experience the West.

COURTESY OF CLACKAMAS MARINE

The Knucklehead Method
(as experienced by the author)

My experience buying a driftboat was a little different. For a couple of months I watched the want ads, observing the prices on the different boats. I was aware that there where three types of materials, and a couple of different sizes. I talked to a few guides and a few salesmen, and some guys who were both salesman and guide. My choices seemed to be aluminum or fiberglass; the used wood boats that I did look at were in pretty sad shape. I wanted a boat that was river ready. I was not looking for a job nor did I want to worry about the boat being damaged during the rocky encounters that I, as a beginner, would surely suffer. Choosing between aluminum and fiberglass was my next challenge. Truthfully, I do not believe that I ever did consciously make that decision.

right. The boat was perfect—all except the paint job.

Truth was, it is not that the paint job was bad, it was in very good shape. And the colors—white, red and, gold—were not bad. The trouble was, this had been the official fishing team boat for a popular beer company. Naturally, it was a floating advertisement. I knew if I did not paint it soon, sounds reminiscent of old beer commercials from TV would follow me around: "Hey, where's the beer" or "No beers around here, they swam that-a-way." (Other fishermen proved me right about that.) I decided that I wanted it, anyway, in spite of the logos.

So, following grandpappy's sound advice, I went home to talk it over with the boss. I begged and I pleaded and I pleaded and I begged—it was embarrassing. I even made promises that I really didn't want to keep—honey dos and the like. Lucky for me, I have a pretty neat lady for a wife—she genuinely wants me

16-Foot Wooden McKenzie

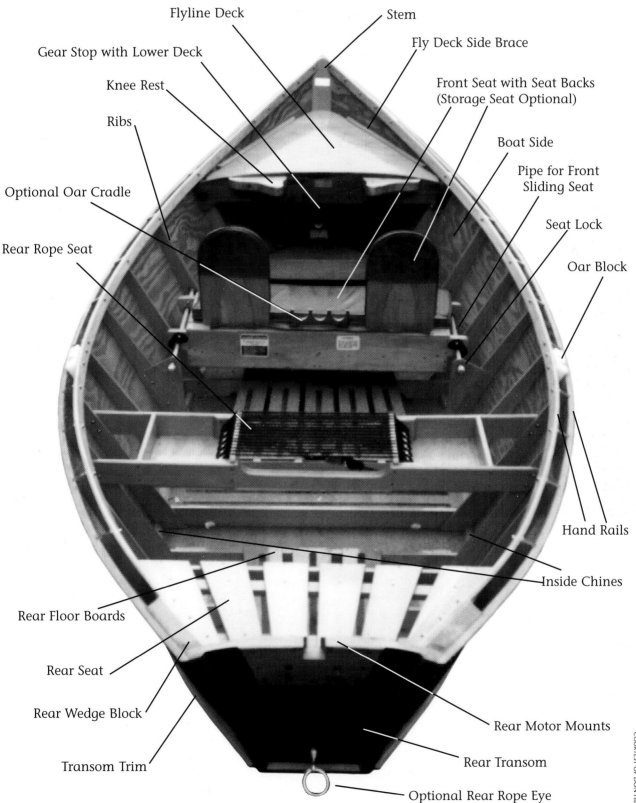

Flyline Deck

Stem

Gear Stop with Lower Deck

Fly Deck Side Brace

Knee Rest

Front Seat with Seat Backs
(Storage Seat Optional)

Ribs

Boat Side

Optional Oar Cradle

Pipe for Front
Sliding Seat

Seat Lock

Rear Rope Seat

Oar Block

Hand Rails

Inside Chines

Rear Floor Boards

Rear Seat

Rear Wedge Block

Rear Motor Mounts

Transom Trim

Rear Transom

Optional Rear Rope Eye

Veltie Pruitt and his good friend and client, Merwin 'Pat' Irish on the Deschutes in this 1938 photo.

COURTESY OF ROY PRUITT

Veltie Pruitt fishing from the first 'light' McKenzie River driftboat.

COURTESY OF ROY PRUITT

Prince Helfrich running Tumwater Falls on the John Day River in a Kaarhus style square-ended Rapid Robert. (Circa 1940)

PHOTOS BY GEORGE GODFREY, COURTESY OF DAVE RODRIGUEZ

Roger Fletcher's model of the Veltie Pruitt 'light' boat.

COURTESY OF PATRICK FARRELL

Boat-builder Bruce Belles on Idaho's South Fork of the Snake. Fall Creek enters the river in a spectacular way. This is a fine way to experience the West.

COURTESY OF CLACKAMAS MARINE

The whitewater pram is another modified driftboat manufactured by several builders. It has a squared bow like a Rapid Robert and a partially squared transom bow like the modern McKenzie driftboat. It is usually built not more than twelve feet long and often it is much shorter. The guys that have them like the light car-topper that can also handle white water.

COURTESY OF KOFLER BOATS

On the South Fork of the Snake, ready to launch.

A fiberglass boat drifting below the Grand Tetons in Wyoming.

Mark Angel running Sherars Falls in the only known driftboat descent of the falls. Do not attempt this fall it could be fatal.

Salvage expert Mark Angel pulls a driftboat up from the depths of the Deschutes River.

Ron Gifford's wooden double-ender.

Try explaining this to the buddy from whom you borrowed it. Whitehorse Rapid victim recovered by Mark Angel.

Driftboater gets out of shape, broaches, and sinks in this tricky rapid called Powerhouse on the upper Clackamas River. Several hours were required to re-float the boat so that, even though slightly damaged, it was able to finish the day's drift.

Dennis Brown pulling off the cushion at the nasty 'Hole In The Wall' rapid on the upper Clackamas.

Roger Fletcher's models of Bob Pritchett's Rogue River Special (bottom) and Zane Grey's boat (top) at Winkle Bar.

Ron Gifford looking over the 'beer boat'.

to enjoy my life. My friends all want one like her. Donna is not only beautiful and intelligent, she pretty much lets me go boating and fishing whenever I get the urge—which is a lot. I still had to agree to keep all of those stupid promises.

The very next evening, right after work, I hustled on over to the boat store to see about making the deal on *my* boat. The used boats were kept out in the yard behind a tall chain link fence. This evening, although the store was open, the gate was locked. I caught the eye of one of the salesmen in the store and was waiting to be helped when a couple of other guys pulled

Eric Kiseda standing in front of the repainted 'beer boat' with a nice summer hatchery fish.

into the lot. They walked up to the locked gate and began to talk about *my* boat.

Suddenly, I wanted that boat about ten times more than when I had pulled in to the store's lot. I knew that I had to act fast or *my* boat would slip away from me. When the salesman came out and asked if he could help us, I was ready. I went on the attack. I was merciless and took no prisoners. "Yes sir," I answered, "I want to buy that beer boat right over there, the red and white one. Put her on a trailer and bring her to me." By George, those interlopers were not going to beat me out of *my* boat.

One of the other fellows got mad, I mean he got real mad. He did not even enter the gate or say a word, but I could hear some unintelligible muttering. Obviously he was not a happy camper. You could tell by the look on his face and the fire in his eyes. He just turned around and left—without a good-bye or even a "kiss my molasses." That was the night I bought my Willie Boat from the owners of Alumaweld. On the way home it occurred to me, "I was going to really have to keep my word and live up to all those stupid promises I had made." What a knucklehead I was.

Prior to looking for a boat, I had not given a lot of thought to outfitting my boat. I got lucky and got good break when I found a complete package and insisted on them throwing in some life jackets. I recommend that you use the scientific method. Define your list of needs and uses, talk to various folks in the know to narrow down your options, and then go look for a deal that meets your list of wants and needs.

Outfitting Your Driftboat

RECENTLY MY BOAT WAS STRIPPED DOWN FOR repairs and painting. My brother and I decided to get in some spur-of-the-moment fishing. When he saw how much gear was needed to get us legal, he was amazed. Everything was necessary, but a lot of it was for just in case.

The following list will help as you begin to set up your boat. Don't be afraid of adding to this list, but consider carefully before you delete any item. This list is in alphabetical order, not in order of importance. Items noted with (*) are required by Coast Guard regulations as of 1999. Regulations change so be sure you have up-to-date information and are operating in compliance with current Coast Guard and State regulations.

Driftboat Equipment and Supplies

Anchor: An appropriate river anchor designed for fast-moving water is the only anchor that should be used. The preferred types are the pyramid, plain ball, or even coffee can-shaped styles are okay. Stay away from fluked or hooked type anchors, you are likely to get them hooked up in fast water and have to cut the line because you cannot pull the anchor up. An anchor stuck in fast water could make you sink.

Anchoring System: The anchoring system should consist of at least one pulley and jam cleat (or a foot release). It should be set up in such a way that the oarsman can raise and lower the anchor without leaving his seat. A dock cleat is handy to secure your anchor so that it will not drop in heavy water. Your anchor rope

Author preparing to release an Umpqua smallmouth bass.

RICK ALSUP

should be three to four times the depth of the water you are fishing. I like 3/8- to 1/2-inch polypropylene. Do not use chain or attempt to anchor over the side of the boat. It is recommended that when going through heavy water you bring the anchor into the boat and eliminate any chance of accidental release.

*Audible Signaling Device: This can be a bell, a horn, or a whistle audible for up to 1/2 mile. Most drift-boaters carry a whistle. There are also some air horns that operate off of compressed air. They are good and loud, but need to have a charged can of air or you get no sound.

Bailing Bucket: This can be a large plastic jug with a good handle that has had the bottom cut out and the lid left on. this works well to scoop up the water. I like to keep a five gallon bucket also which doubles as anchor rope storage.

Boat Repair Kit: This kit should contain some basic repair items to ensure that you can keep going should you pop a seam or punch a hole in your hull. See the repair kit checklist in Chapter 10 for a detailed list of items for your repair kit.

Bow line: The bowline is a short tag line for short dura-tion tie-offs, put-ins, and take-outs. You do not need much more than 15 to 20 feet.

Carabiners: At least three or four of the twist-locking type carabiners are useful for fastening lines and other items. In an emergency they can be used much like a pulley system when rigged in Z-drag fashion to rescue a broached boat or an entrapped swimmer.

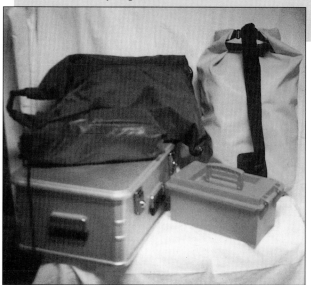

Assortment of dry bags and boxes.

Dry Bags and Boxes: There is quite an assortment of bags and boxes commercially available that do an excellent job of protecting your gear, clothing, and dry goods.

First-Aid Kit: See the checklist in Chapter 10 for a detailed list of first-aid kit items. It is a good idea to be certified in first aid and CPR. Encourage your river friends to get certified as well. Certification is inexpensive and uses up only one day every two years.

Flashlight and Spare Batteries: A flashlight is the least amount of light required after dark for use as a navigation marker. It is always possible to get caught out late, so a good flashlight and spare batteries are a good idea anyway. The flashlight is to mark your posi-tion for other boats to see. Do not expect to navigate a river by flashlight. You just can't see far enough ahead. The river absorbs the light.

Safety gear: rope, carabiners and cord for Prusik Loops.

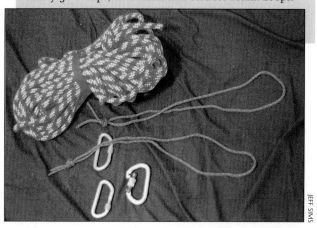

JEFF SIMS

Ice Chest: A good-quality cooler is required to keep your water and perishables cold. It's also handy to ice down your catch of the day.

*Night Lighting: If your driftboat is equipped with an outboard motor, and you are using it (the motor) after dark , you are required to have the standard naviga-tion lights—a red/green light on the bow and a white one mounted on a short mast on the stern. If you are non-motorized, a good flashlight will meet the require-ments.

Oar Rubbers or Stops: These are made to keep your oars from sliding out of the oarlocks and into the drink. You will need one for each oar, plus a spare.

*Oars (3-4): Always carry at least one spare oar. On a float through wild country or heavy rapids, contempo-rary wisdom favors carrying at least two spare oars.

Oars are made of wood, aluminum, or composites of graphite and plastic. You will need oars that are fit-ted to you, the boat, and the oarlocks. Choosing the right set of oars is a personal decision based upon your own needs. Rather than try to present all of the pros and cons of the different materials, I am going to point out a couple of observations. You must look at the prices, the use you will put them to, and the time you spend rowing.

After talking with several guides whom row two-hundred-plus days a year, recurrent qualities keep popping up: Materials, length, blade weight and width, flex and feel. The length of your oars can be critical, especially in fast water. The different materials affect all of the following qualities to one degree or another and have varying life spans. Oars that are a little too short are better than oars that are a little too long, especially in fast water. Blade width and weight can make a lot of difference to the feel of the oar. Flex is needed to act as a shock absorber between you and the water, feel is a combination of balance and weight.

Choosing a particular material for the oars and blades is an individual decision made based upon your needs and the type of water you will be working. Most of us need to consult with our bosses and wallets also. The choices include: Several varieties of wood—ash, spruce, and fir are popular. Fiberglass, aluminum, or graphite compositions with plastic blades have found a market as well. Blade width and thickness varies from five to 10 inches wide while the thickness of the blade can run from 1/8 inch all the way up to more than 1/2 inch. Your choices will, again, depend upon your needs and the advice you receive.

The length of the oar is a little more difficult to determine, as there are many variables that need to be considered. Perhaps mathematicians will some day come up with a formula that will allow for all those variables. Those variables that must be considered are: the width of your boat, the alignment of your seat in relation to your oarlocks, the height of your seat, and the length of your back from your butt to your shoulders. Another valid consideration is the type of water in which you are planning to play. Will it be broad open water or tough, fast technical water with narrow chutes and channels?

The flex of the oar will save tremendously on the stress and wear rowing puts on your wrists, elbows, and shoulder. If you are a weekend boater, you may never notice the differences. On the other hand, if you are a professional who must row all day long every working day, you will notice and probably want to save yourself as much suffering possible.

The feel of an oar is subtle and determined by the way it works with the water and by the weight and stress inflicted upon your wrists, elbows, and shoulders. Each type of oar has a slightly different feel based upon the materials of which it is made. This feel includes the weight that you feel while rowing. It also includes the way that the position or attitude of the oar can be determined without the need to see it.

You cannot accurately judge how well an oar will work for you without actually trying it. You can test the balance by balancing an oar over a chair. A well-balanced oar will feel lighter than an unbalanced one. For example an oar that is blade heavy will inflict more

A matter of life or death: Make sure you are using the currect PFD. Check the Coast Guard Regulations.

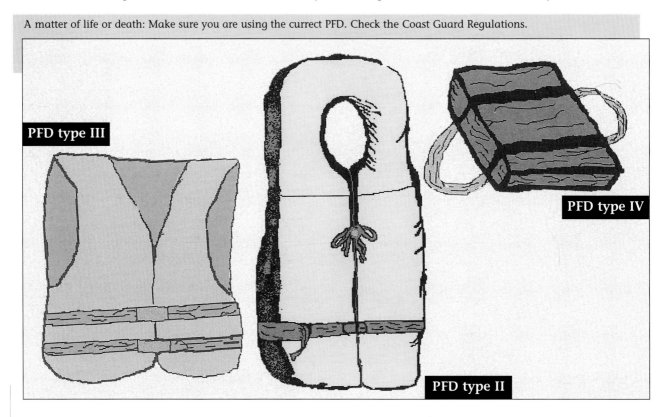

PFD type III

PFD type IV

PFD type II

stress and fatigue upon you. The fatigue you feel at the end of a long day's rowing will be directly proportional to how heavy those oars feel. Finding a dealer that will work with you is going to be important if you are going to be spending a lot of time on the sticks.

The novice oarsman will probably not realize a difference in the feel and action of the various oars. This is something that will come when he has had quite a bit of time on the river. Initially, he should be just as satisfied with one oar as another. On the other hand, experienced professionals seem to favor good-quality wood oars made of ash or spruce. Spruce is the lightest and most flexible of the two, but is harder to come by and more expensive because of the unavailability of good-quality wood. Of course there are professionals and outfitters who are happy with the composites and aluminum oars. As I stated previously, the choice will be yours.

You will have to spend some time investigating the attributes of the various materials used in the oars currently on the market and of course you will have your wallet concerns as well. Just as some time and investigation go into picking out the driftboat that is right for you, so also is the case when choosing the oars. Read the manufacturer's literature, talk to old hands and dealers. Experiment with several different types out on the water. You will arrive at the right kind of oar for yourself.

Oarlocks (3) and Spare Pins: Most boats come equipped with heavy brass oarlocks. You want to be sure that yours are bent together at the top just enough

so your oar cannot be lifted out of it. You want them just tight enough to hold the oar in, but loose enough so that if an oar gets jammed up, it will pop out instead of breaking the oarlock. A jammed-up oar can capsize your boat if it will not pop out of the oarlock. A lost pin can mean that you may lose an oarlock overboard. I can assure you from experience that they do not float.

*Personal Flotation Devices (one for each occupant, plus a spare): PFDs are required by law, one for each occupant and a spare. Children 16 and under must wear their life preserver (now called a Personal Flotation Device). All boats 16 feet and over are also required to carry a TYPE IV (seat cushion type) throwable device.

The best PFDs currently available for heavy rapids (Class III International scale or Class V Western scale) are the type V commercial whitewater PFDs that are really a modified type III personal flotation device. This type of PFD has a collar designed to help keep a swimmer's head above the surface. Crotch straps are an excellent way to ensure that the PFD stays on. Type III PFDs, while worn by many whitewater enthusiasts, are intended for general boating activities that require more freedom of movement, like fishing and canoeing. They are not specifically designed for conditions found in rough water. Type II U-shaped PFDs are appropriate for calm-water-use only. Type IV PFDs are throwable devices, like seat cushions or rings.

U.S. Coast Guard regulations require that all watercraft carry one Type III or better PFD per person and

Type V life jackets (PFDs, front and back view).

one type IV throwable device, and that they be readily available. ("Readily available" means you can get to your PFD in an emergency; it does not mean leave it in its original package or locked in a dry box.) In rough water your PFD should be worn at all times. It is also recommended that an extra PFD be carried when running whitewater or when on extended trips. PFDs should be size-fitted to each individual and children should wear child-sized life jackets. All should state Coast Guard Approved with an approval number. If you expect a life jacket to save you, you must be wearing it.

Plugs (2): Plugging the drain hole in your driftboat is kind of important if you don't like to sit in the river. Keep the extra plug in your repair kit. They are not expensive and usually last for years, but they do occasionally wear out, break, or get lost.

Portable Toilet: Several rivers now and, it is rumored, more in the future, will have regulations in place that requiring you to pack it out. There are several toilets on the market. Check the river management plan for the sanitation requirements of the river section you are planning to float. This will help to assure that you purchase an approved system.

Prussic Loops (2): Prusik Loops are used as breaks with Z-drag systems on lines used to pull boats off rocks and to rescue folks entrapped in the river.

Throw Bag Rescue Rope (60 feet): These bags of rope are a slick way to heave a line to a passenger or anyone else overboard and in trouble. Accurately throwing a rope 40 to 60 feet or more from a heaving boat is much harder than it looks. It pays to practice throwing rescue ropes. A rescue bag is faster to get into play than a coiled line. If you have to re-throw it, just coil the line—it's too slow to re-stuff the bag.

100-Foot Rope: This is multi-use rope. You can use it to tie up at night, line rapids, or maybe to help yourself or someone else be pulled off a rock. Make sure it is a good stout rope. (3/8 to 5/8 braided polypropylene is an excellent choice.) Stow it away. You do not want your rope to become a danger itself.

Sanitation Kit: Recommended items include: toilet paper (stored in a Ziploc bag); a shovel to bury the evidence; waterless hand cleaner or biodegradable soap; and small garbage bags for waste toilet paper, etc.

Sea Anchor: A sea anchor can be used to prevent yawing, or swaying, in fast current. I have used a variety of items to act as a sea anchor or stabilizer including a towel, burlap fish bag, and a Class IV PFD (seat-cushion type). Note: It is not safe to anchor in too fast a current.

Seating: Most boats have wood or plastic swivel seats that mount on the benches for passengers and either a rope/web or tractor seat for the oarsman.

A Z-drag system doubles the strength of your pull when pulling a boat off a broach.

JEFF SIMS

Storage: Most boat builders consider storage and make it available. Custom boxes are often incorporated into the benches used for seating. You may wish to add to or rearrange the storage provided with your boat. There are some nice plastic boxes that are fairly water tight, or you can have custom aluminum dry boxes built.

Survival Kit: If you are close to town where a rescue would happen in a very short time, one survival kit per boat may be sufficient. If you are in wild country where rescue could take a day or more, one survival kit per occupant should be included. It should be easily accessible, waterproof, and buoyant. A suggested contents list is included in the checklists section of Chapter 10.

Water Supply: You will be safe assuming that the water in our Northwest waters is never safe to drink. A parasite picked up in the river can give you a real case

On the South Fork of the Snake, ready to launch.

of the galloping GIs and cause severe abdominal pain and other nasty symptoms; *Giardia* can be fatal. It is recommended that you pack and use a filter to replenish your drinking water when clean tap or bottled water is not readily available. Drinking plenty of water is a good habit to practice at all times and is particularly important while on the river. It will help prevent or at least fight fatigue and you need to be replenishing those body fluids lost to perspiration, even on cold days.

By including the items in this list, you should be well prepared for safe, comfortable drifting. You will also be in compliance with the Coast Guard regulations. Remember, no one plans on mishaps, but many fail to plan. If you are prepared you will be more likely to recover from a mishap.

Fish on! Duped by a fly.

CHAPTER 7

The Basics of Rowing

ROWING IS MORE THAN A SKILL, IT IS AN ART, AN exercise that with time and practice melds the mind, body, and the oars into the motion and intricacies of the waters. The expert oarsman has achieved a state of being in which his oars have become an extension of his arms and he has attained a heightened awareness and understanding of the undulations of the river and its currents. The novice seeks the same: To become one with the oars and to be in tune with the water. No book can give that to you. Only much time on the water—countless days on the sticks—will make you an expert oarsman.

Here are some basic tools to help you get started in the right direction:

First, adjust the seat and the oars to fit you. Adjust your seat so that it is about 12 to 18 inches behind the oarlocks. If you have an adjustable foot bar, adjust it so that when sitting in the oarsman's seat your legs are slightly bent. When you are pulling hard on the oars, extending your legs against the foot bar will help you get your back into it. In heavy water you want all the power you can muster.

Your oars need to be adjusted so that the handles are just slightly apart. A couple of inches to start. You may want to adjust them out as far as 6 to 8 inches after you have worked with them for a while.

Driftboats in Big Sky Country near Jackson, Wyoming.

COURTESY OF CLACKAMAS MARINE

You can learn to row all by yourself. It doesn't take a genius but it does take some time. Being too macho and moving too fast presents some very real dangers. If you take passengers you will be subjecting them to the results of any mistakes you make and you can be held legally and financially accountable. You should be rowing your own boat so that if you get a few dents, maybe a seam that needs to be re-welded, a sunk

Serious pulling is required to avoid the big hole in Martin's Creek Rapid. This takes some knowledge and skill. It is not a safe place for a beginner to practice.

COURTESY OF KOFFLER BOATS

COURTESY OF KOFFLER BOATS

boat—you get the picture—no one will be really upset at you. It is recommended that you start out a little slower. Learn to row still water before you try moving water.

To illustrate the point of getting in over your head, the picture on page 41 demonstrates graphically the awesome destructive power of a river moving through a Class IV rapid. Attempting water beyond your ability could result in a tragic ending. This boat was brand new and the owner was an experienced oarsman with some knowledge of the river. He just didn't have enough practice on the oars in that kind of water. Slowly working your way up the scale of difficulty will help you avoid having a boat end up like this.

This driftboat sank in Whitehorse. It's on display near Maupin on the way to a popular Deschutes River put in.

Find a calm place to begin your rowing. I know you want to get out where the fish are and I know you want to run the white water, but wait. A small lake or pond will do. So will a slow, meandering stream. This will be your place to practice until you can easily row steady for a couple of hours and execute the following maneuvers without thinking about the mechanics involved. In the middle of a big rapid with a nasty obstacle in front of you there is no time to think: "Okay, now I have to spin to the right so let's see, if I push with the right . . ." "Your actions must come as naturally and as automatically as walking.

When you are rowing, you will have an oar in each hand. Each oar will always be doing something. While pulling the right oar to effect a right turn, the left oar can be held up out of the water to let the right work alone or it can be pushed to assist the turn. You can drag one oar while you row with the other to steady the boat as you ride an eddy fence or the right oar can be pushed to assist the left oar pulling for a left turn. These movements, while not difficult to perform, are quite awkward at first. If you stay at it long enough, they will become automatic and require no conscious thought when executing them.

The ABCs of Rowing

The Galloway Position: The oarsman faces downstream. The end of the boat that faces downstream is not relevant to the position.

Rowing Forward: This method of rowing is called the portegee. The motion is pushing. It is commonly used to move the boat forward. It is also used to increase speed during downstream travel, sometimes to push through a big wave, sometimes just to make sure you enter a slot when the current is trying to move you off your mark.

Forward Ferry: Rowing forward towards your goal. In calmer and slower waters it sometimes will be used for minor maneuvering.

Rowing Backwards: The motion is pulling. It is the standard method used to row a rowboat. Usually the oarsman's back is to the bow. In the driftboat we will point our backs downstream (bow down) and row when we are trying to make time against an upstream wind or a slow current.

Backferry: The backferry is the driftboater's most important maneuver. It is used to line up the boat for the correct entry to a rapids and to pull around obstacles. It is also used to hold the boat back against the current to allow the passengers who are fishing an opportunity to thoroughly cover the water or to hold back a diver and bait or allow a plug to work. Once the basic movement is understood, backferrying is not difficult. The basic premise is: Point at what you do not want to hit

Veltie Pruitt works his way through a Deschutes River boulder garden in 1938. Prince Helfrich and Pat Irish look on.

COURTESY OF ROY PRUITT

and row backwards. Keep as shallow an angle to the current as possible, and row backwards to pull yourself from where you do not want to be. You will move opposite of your front, backing the boat into position.

This expert oarsman demonstrates the Galloway method of pulling away from where you don't want to be (backferrying) as he skirts the edge.

Turning the Boat

Right turn pulled.

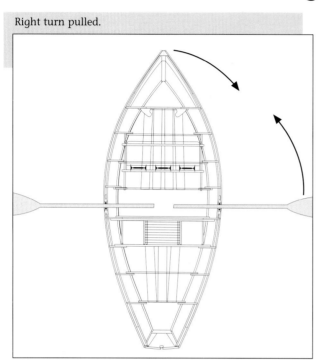

Left turn pulled.

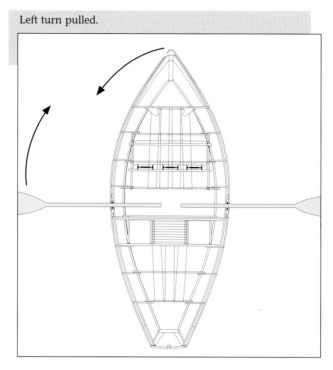

Right turn pushed.

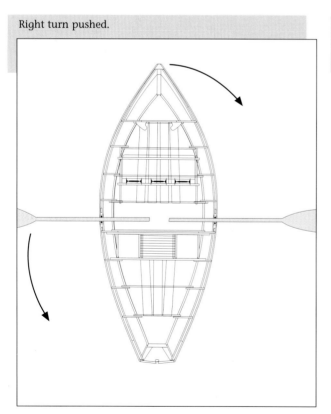

Left turn pushed.

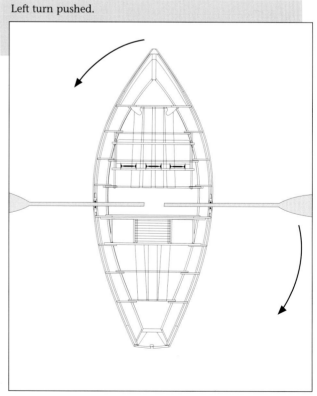

Right Turn: Pulling on the right oar or pushing on the left oar will turn the bow to the right. It will not move the boat right.

Left Turn: Pulling on the left oar or pushing on the right oar will turn the bow to the left. It will not move the boat left.

Double Oar Turns: These two turns are powerful and fast. They are used to spin the boat as little or as much as needed. Sometimes they are used to spin your boat back after a whirlpool has spun it or you've just cartwheeled off a rock you hit head on. Sometimes they are needed just to hold the boat's attitude or keep you from spinning in heavy water. Most oarsmen develop the good habit of using a double oar turn for almost every turn. Being able to react automatically with this turn can be a boat saver.

Right double oar turn.

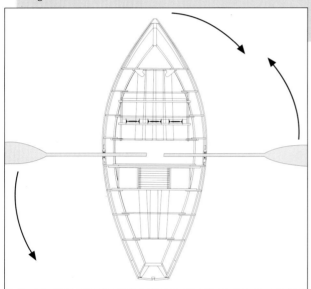

Right Double Oar Turn: Push with your left oar and pull with your right.

Right double oar turn.

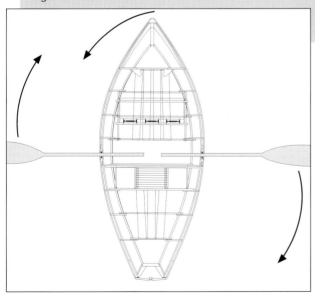

Left Double Oar Turn: Push with your right oar and pull with your left.

Driftboat in the big water of Colorado rapid on the Deschutes River.

ERIC BIGLER

You will find that working a boat in current is very different from the placid water of a lake. The current will sometimes amplify, and at other times diminish, the effect you have with your oars. Practice rowing upstream, against the current. Look for eddies along the edge of the river where the current is flowing upstream and practice using them to move upstream. Now is the time to start to understand the river and its currents. Figure it out and become one with the current, use its strength to make your job easier. Do not fight it. Use it to pull your boat to where you want it to go. If it is too strong and there is no eddy, you can tack back and forth across the river angling upstream. Work along the edges of the river where there is less current. If you find a few midstream obstacles, wonderful. Work your way around them with your backferry, you can rest for a moment in the eddies they create.

My river rat friend and fishing buddy, Lee Haslet, recommends watching objects like sticks float through the rapids to learn the way that the currents work. Toss driftwood sticks into the river at various places and watch what happens. Where does the current take it and what does the current do with it? Eventually you will be able to predict the path a stick will take from any given point. Gaining this understanding of the flow will help you guide your boat through using, rather than fighting, the current.

Leroy 'Roy' Pruitt, who has spent about 60 years guiding on the McKenzie River, developed a unique method of teaching rowing to his university extension school students. Using a diagram of a boat on the river he was able to effectively explain how a boat works its way around an obstacle using the backferry. He learned the principles of backing a boat down the river as a child playing along the McKenzie in side channels and creeks with a toy boat.

With a couple of strings attached in the middle of his toy boat, (attached at about the same point the oarlocks are found on a full-size boat), Pruitt found that he could back his toy downstream and around obstacles by pulling on one or both strings just enough to simulate the action of rowing with the backferry.

Negotiating Hazards or Obstacles

Obstacles are best avoided by following the basic rules of rowing a driftboat:

1. Aim at what you do not want to hit or where you don't want to be and row backward—backferry.
2. Set up ahead of time and let the river do as much of the work as it will.

Plan your course around obstacles and through mazes well ahead of time. Position your boat so the current does most of the work with you holding the boat on course, pushing through big waves and providing minor course changes.

Negotiating The Stretch of Water in Figure 1.

1. Enter rapid on tongue (A). Be aware of hole/ reversal (B).
2. Make sure to stay off rock(C). Pull away, but not too much. You don't want to get to far left or you'll have to contend with the side curlers coming off the bank (D).
3. Start pulling to stay off cushion (E).
4. Pull away from the cushion (E) to catch the top of the eddy (F).
5. Swing downstream to ride eddy fence (or boil line) (G).
6. Pull to start ferry to avoid cushion and log (H).
7. Ferry more strongly, pulling up and away from the log at (H).
8. A few more pulls then swing to catch the downstream flow.
9. Pull now to slow your momentum, put on the brakes.
10. Swing sharply to get position to pull off the rock (J). And to be able to catch the eddy (K) behind the log (H).
11. Finally, you can swing the bow downstream to drop through the chute (I) and enjoy the ride through the tail waves.

Figure 1. Working a driftboat through and around obstacles.

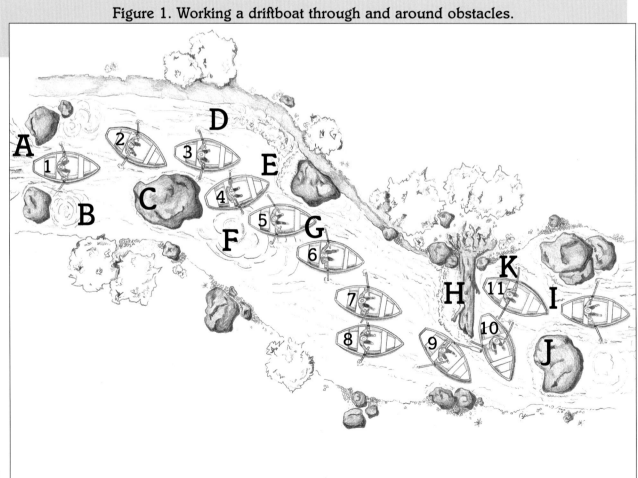

BRIAN GRIFITHS

Leroy 'Roy' Pruitt began guiding on the McKenzie when he was 14 years old. In this photo, taken about 1962, in a contemporary Hindman-style boat, Roy treats some 'dudes' (paying clients) to Chuck Hole rapid on Idaho's River of No Return—Middle Fork of the Salmon River. This river requires expert oarsmanship.

New boats at the launch site waiting to go on a test drive.

CHAPTER 8

Reading the Water

"Learning to 'read the water' was the best education a whitewater man could have."

The Rogue: A River to Run
by Florence Arman

ALMOST ANY RIVER IN THE WEST HAS DANGERS lurking both above and below the surface. These dangers are usually visible to the trained eye, but to the untrained eye, not all are obvious or recognizable as being as dangerous as they are. Learning what the various features of a river are, having the ability to discern their respective dangers, and knowing how to find safe passage, sometimes how to find any passage, is an ability that comes with time on the water. I will help you learn what the various river features are, how to identify them, and help you start, in the most basic manner, learning to discern the danger of any particular feature.

The ability to "read water" will come if you follow the dictates of common sense as you spend time on the river studying its moods, motions, and currents in relation to all of its features. Practice all you can on easy rivers, moving up the scale of difficulty gradually. Join groups, find friends and organizations that will allow you to tag along so that you may gain your experience among seasoned boatmen and move up the scale of difficulty in good company.

Glen Wooldridge discussed reading the water in *The Rogue: A River to Run* by Florence Arman:

"There are several things about the water that tell you what is going on underneath, where the danger is. The color of the water, its motion, density, and sounds all tell you part of the story. You have to pay close attention to them, because your life and the others in the boat all depend on it.

"There will be black, slick places; frothy whitewater; more dense whitewater; rapids; riffles; currents; falls; swirls and eddies; chutes and bends.

"Slick, glassy water is sometimes dead water, but at other times it is swift rapids. It takes an experienced riverman to tell the difference before he gets into it. Frothy whitewater is full of air caused by the pounding of the water over a riverbed full of boulders. It is thin water and can't be run. Whitewater that is more dense is over deeper boulders and you can run it. Fast, smooth water is deep and navigable.

"You can tell the depth of a boulder under fast-moving water by the motion of the water over it. The wake of the water, over the boulder, tells its position underneath the surface.

"A wave doesn't necessarily mean rocks; it can be just the speed of the river's current. Decisions must be made fast and constantly as to which whitewater is runable. There isn't always a clear open channel to follow. In fact in most whitewater rivers, there seldom is an open channel."

In order to read water you must have an understanding of the river features and characteristics. The following pages are no substitute for time on the river, but they can give you a short cut to learning the names and some initial understanding of the river features and their characteristics.

Netting a fall chinook from a fiberglass modified McKenzie driftboat.

COURTESY OF LAVRO BOATS

A Brief Description of Typical River Features

"Your Action:" ▶ Indicates the actions a driftboater usually would or should take.

◀ **Bend in the River:** While not difficult to see or understand, bends in the river have typical characteristics and dynamics you should understand. Usually the deepest water is on the outside of the bend where the strongest current will be found. The outside of the bend is where the biggest potential for trouble will be. That is where debris like logs may stack up. Also, depending upon the gradient and the tightness of the corner, you may find the current pushing you into the bank, which is usually high, and possibly into side curler-type waves. Sometimes a boulder or even a root wad on the outside of a corner can be situated in such a way that the water will wash right up on it creating a huge cushion with an upstream eddy and a downstream hole. The bend is usually further complicated by shallows on the inside of the curve and eddies with a boil line that can be quite strong and dangerous. The hydraulics in a bend can be hair-raising. (See "Broach" on page 48.)

Your Action: ▶ Start into the corner as far to the inside as you can, it is very easy to let the current push you to the outside if need be, but some pretty strong rowing against the strongest current will be required to move you from the outside back to the inside of the corner, it may even be impossible to row against the current in some situations. Oftentimes you may be required to ride the eddy fence (boil line) around the tightest part of the curve until you can straighten out and catch the main current and the standing waves.

◀ **Big Water:** This is generally deep, fast, and very turbulent water with huge waves, ten feet high or higher. Boats here, even under control, can look and feel like little toys being tossed about in a bathtub occupied by a rambunctious child. This kind of water is found on the Colorado, the Snake, and to a lesser degree on the Deschutes during normal flows. It can be found on many rivers during very high water.

Your Action: ▶ You must be competent on the oars in order to maintain shape (boat's attitude in relation to the current and obstacles) and keep from being swamped or rolled. Push through the big waves. Even a

Drawing of a typical river bend.

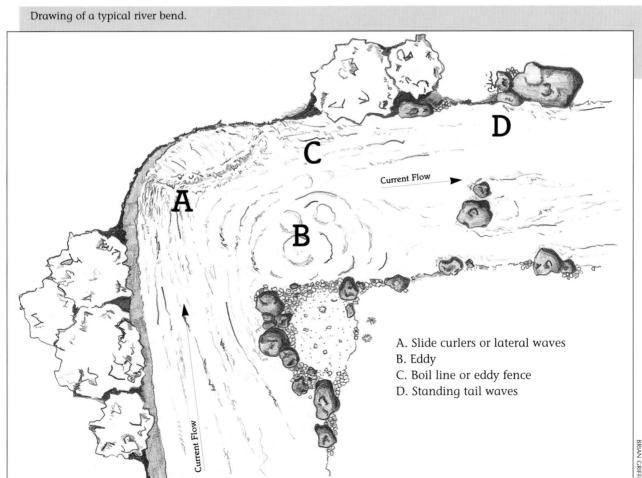

A. Slide curlers or lateral waves
B. Eddy
C. Boil line or eddy fence
D. Standing tail waves

pointed stern will not totally eliminate the possibility of stalling and capsizing.

◄ **Boils:** Upwelling of water usually found along eddy lines and irregular cliffs where the current is swift and strong and the water deep and turbulent. This water can be tricky to maneuver or row in and severe boils and whirlpools can combine to capsize your boat.

Your Action: Make sure that your boat is well trimmed (balanced evenly from side to side and front to back), keep the center of gravity over the eddy line and react swiftly when your boat is pulled down or up on one side or the other. Be ready to shift the weight of yourself and passengers if necessary.

Driftboater gets out of shape, broaches, and sinks in this tricky rapid called Powerhouse on the upper Clackamas River. Several hours were required to re-float the boat so that, even though slightly damaged, it was able to finish the day's drift.

◄ **Broach:** A situation where a boat has hung up on an obstruction, often sideways to the current, and is pinned there by that current. There is the danger of the upstream end or side of the boat being sucked under water and the boat sinking.

Your Action: Generally a broach will result in the evacuation of personnel and gear followed by rope

work to recover the boat (see Chapter Ten: Trouble on the River). Many times the current will eventually wash the boat off the rock and proceed to sink it as happened in the previous two photos. The powerful hydraulics of the river frequently will combine to severely damage the hull. In this case, recovery may require an expert salvage man.

Broaching can result in the need for the services of a good 'salvage' man.

◄ **Boulder Garden:** A boulder-choked piece of water requiring expert maneuvering through very technical water. Blossom Bar on the Rogue River is a classic example of a boulder garden.

Blossom Bar from upstream. A classic boulder garden. This section of Class IV water is a delight to run as long as you make no critical mistakes.

Your Action: You must be competent on the sticks, be able to maintain a cool head, and have the ability to plan an entire route ahead with just one glance, and yet be flexible enough to improvise if your first plan doesn't work and you find yourself having difficulty finding a clear passage.

◄ **CFS (cubic feet per second):** The volume of water currently moving downstream is measured in CFS.

Oarsmanship in the boulder garden on the upper Clackamas River.

◄ **Channel:** The part of the river that is a path of water flowing downstream. In any given stretch there may be many channels or as few as only one.

◄ **Chute:** A constricted channel that is fairly narrow in relation to the main body of water. Chutes are usually fast little drops. Sometimes chutes are the only passage that you will find through a rock or boulder garden.

Emmett Heath, a professional guide, brings his driftboat through a narrow chute in the rocky chasm that is Utah's Flaming Gorge.

◄ **Cushion:** The mass of water that stacks up against an obstacle that is extending above the water line. It is a backflow off the obstacle.

Your Action: Use your strong backferry in conjunction with that backflow to hold your boat off the obstacle when otherwise you would be pushed right into it by the current.

Drawing of a cushion.

Current Flow

Dennis Brown pulling off the cushion at the nasty 'Hole in the Wall' rapid on the upper Clackamas.

◄ **Curlback:** The portion of a reversal that is actually an above-surface wave curling back upstream.
◄ **Curler:** Usually a standing wave that crests and breaks back over on itself. It can mark a big hole or be a fairly benign standing tail wave.
Your Action: You must decide whether to go over the curler or around it. Be careful; large curlers can turn your boat upside down in a heartbeat.
◄ **Current:** The flow of water, the strength of which is determined by the gradient and volume of the flow.
◄ **Drop:** A significant lowering of the river's surface altitude measured over any distance. Usually in terms of river running, the gradient of the river or the amount of vertical descent in a falls or a rapid is called the drop.

Over the drop. This rapid (Powerhouse on the upper Clackamas) has a fair-sized drop to get you started.

◄ **Eddy:** A flow of water opposite to the main current creating a circular motion of water.. The upstream flow of water can be either horizontal as in a whirlpool or vertical as in a reversal. (See "Reversal.") Examples could be an extreme whirlpool strong enough to sink a driftboat, a back flow downstream off a small above-surface rock or obstruction, or a huge lazy section of deep slow water that you sometimes find on a big slow bend of the river. Normally, the deeper the pool and the slower the current, the less dangerous an eddy will be. The volume of flow, the speed of the main current, the presence of a deep pool, and the geological formations along the banks and bottom of the river all contribute to what form the eddy takes.

Your Action: Pay attention to where the eddies are and study them. Tight eddies in conjunction with a strong current can be extremely difficult to row out of. White eddies behind rocks can be a nice spot to rest in or to fish as the eddy will hold you without too much help on your part. See the diagram of a typical river bend, page 47.

◄ **Eddy Line/Fence:** A distinctive band of boily looking water that marks the boundary between water moving upstream from water moving downstream. It is not unusual for there to be a marked difference in surface level of the water between the upstream and downstream flows of water.

Your Action: Oftentimes you will have to ride the eddy fence to move past an eddy on one side and some other river obstacle on the other. I find this situation on fast, tight river bends. When you are moving along an eddy fence it is not uncommon to row with one oar and drag the other to keep from being spun around by whirlpools.

◄ **Entry:** The beginning of a predetermined route through a rapid. The entry may be a rock gate and/or a well-defined "V" pointing your way.

◄ **Falls:** Either a steep cascade or free-fall, an abrupt vertical drop, as the river dives over a cliff, ledge, or boulder mass.

Your Action: Most runable falls are steep cascades and most are dangerous. Most falls are runable in driftboats only by experts or not at all. Do not attempt to run a falls until you have been certified—either as an expert or insane. Both descriptions work.

A chinook salmon fights its way up Rainy Falls on the wild Rogue River. Driftboats generally opt to skip this 10- to 12-foot drop and wild reversal by lining their boats through a side channel called the fish ladder on the opposite side of the river. A narrow side channel was blasted to make lining fairly easy.

Dennis Brown riding the tail waves below Carter Falls, an exciting Class IV rapid on the Clackamas River.

Prince Helfrich running Tumwater Falls on the John Day River in a Kaarhus-style square-ended Rapid Robert. (Circa 1940)

PHOTOS BY GEORGE GODFREY, COURTESY OF DAVE RODRIGUEZ

◀ **Flat Water:** Unclasssed water without rapids or big waves. Mishaps involving driftboats often occur on flat water due to a failure to maintain vigilance. Floating obstacles, other boats, and careless occupants have been known to tip boats over.

Your Action: Even though it is easy going, maintain your vigilance. Keep a sharp eye out for debris and other boats. Do not let your passengers get too unruly just because the water looks kind.

◀ **Frog Water:** Slow, often deep, flat water that will require you to row if you want to get anywhere soon is referred to as 'frog' water.

◀ **Gate:** A narrow passageway that is generally navigated as safe passage, often the entrance to a rapid or particular stretch of river.

◀ **Gradient:** The drop in surface altitude of a river. It is generally measured in footage of decrease per river mile, i.e., this river drops about 78 feet per mile.

◀ **Haystack:** A large standing wave. It may be created by an under-the-surface obstacle or by fast-moving water colliding with slow water.

Your Action: Be careful in evaluating this feature. Your best bet is to avoid running a haystack that you do not know about. The haystack in the next photo has a nasty rock tooth that helps create it. Driftboats and rafts alike have run it successfully. On the other hand a man I know smashed in the hull on a new aluminum driftboat on that rock. That was the end of his driftboating days. Use caution.

Haystack wave in McIver Falls on the lower Clackamas River has a nasty rock spike in the middle of it. In high water you can go over, but not without some risk of dumping. In low water the rock is exposed and easy to avoid. At a moderate level, the rock can be a sleeper—it will definitely wake you up when it finds you.

◀ **Heavy Water:** Deep turbulent water with great big waves and very strong hydrostatic forces at work. Good examples are Colorado and Rattlesnake Rapids on Central Oregon's Deschutes River.

Prince Helfrich in big water on the Middle Fork of the Salmon. Being totally surrounded by heavy water like this can be a little intimidating.

COURTESY OF DAVE HELFRICH

◄ **Hog Trough:** A big hole followed by a sizable reversal. A boat eater.

◄ **Hole:** A hole occurs after a drop over a boulder or ledge just above a reversal. The bigger the drop, the bigger the reversal. The bigger the hole, the more dangerous the resulting reversal.

> *Your Action:* ▶ Large holes, hog troughs, or reversals should be avoided. Smaller ones are runable especially if your passengers need a shower. Push hard on the oars to power through them. See "Reversal."

◄ **Hydraulic:** Hydraulic is an adjective transformed by river people into a noun. It is used to name the extreme turbulence associated with powerful hydrostatic pressure that is created when a high volume of water is funneled into a narrow passage over a good-sized drop. Extreme river features such as reversals, boils and whirlpools, large irregular waves, and severe side currents are the kinds of extreme turbulence called hydraulics.

> *Your Action:* ▶ Strong hydraulics usually mean that you should be pretty good on the sticks. Extreme hydraulics should be avoided in a driftboat.

◄ **Keeper:** A reversal that is strong enough to hold boats or swimmers for a measurable period of time. Often keepers will look quite innocent but have the potential to be extremely dangerous. They are found immediately below river-wide cross-current ledges and low head dams. These types of reversals can hold a boat for quite a while and be extremely dangerous. Boats coming up river that have gotten too close to low head dams and cross-current ledges have been known to have been pulled into the hole and capsize.

In 1999 this very thing happened to a powerful jet boat at Willamette Falls. When it went down, the river claimed a life.

Large holes/reversals can also be keepers. Be wary of reversals big enough or powerful enough to be keepers.

> *Your Action:* ▶ Avoid big holes altogether, especially the kind that can be keepers. If you have any doubts about any river feature, avoid it.

◄ **Ledges:** A geologic strata that can run either parallel or at any degree up to perpendicular to the current. A ledge with an upstream hollow underneath that is only partially perpendicular to the current can be a trap for swimmers. Ledges, mixed with water speed and a high volume or CFS and big drops, can be responsible for extreme hydraulics.

> *Your Action:* ▶ Ledge situations need to be studied thoroughly prior to any attempt to run them. If possible, watch other boats to see how their oarsmen deal with this feature. Look for places below the ledge where the water is shooting over at no more than about a 45-degree angle. Avoid ledges that meet or bisect the current at more than 45 degrees. Exercise extreme caution. See Keeper.

◄ **Narrows:** A section of river marked by constricted passage, frequently caused by narrow channels among steep cliffs. It is not uncommon for narrows to have deeper water than the average river depth. Narrows can be scary, especially if they are long and you must ship or pull in your oars. Once those oars are in, all you can do is fasten your seatbelts (PFDs) and hang on for the ride (or for dear life).

Mule Creek canyon on the wild-and-scenic Rogue is a narrows that contains the Coffeepot, a rounded depression in the cliff wall that creates a wild swirling and boiling witch's cauldron of whirlpools. This is one of the most incredible places in the world. It has both the power to terrify and enchant. Sometimes it will hold a boat for ten minutes or so until an upwelling creates a surge that just pushes you on out. Sometimes you slide right on through without a care.

DONNA ALSUP

Oarsmen get a chance to take a breather and collect their thoughts once they reach this spot in the narrows of the upper Clackamas.

DENNIS BROWN

A pillow is simply a mound of water over an object. Sometimes it is followed by small standing waves.

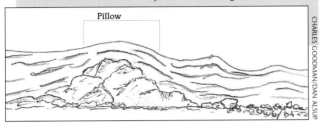

◄ **Pillow:** A pillow is a mound of water caused by a boulder laying just below the surface. If the boulder is down deep enough, your boat can slide harmlessly over the top, if not, the banging of the bottom of your hull will wake you up or at least get your attention. A rooster tail below what appears to be a pillow could indicate a pour-over rock followed by a fair-sized reversal. Better check it out before running it.

◄ **Pool:** A section of river that is usually deeper and slower than the average of that river. In Oregon's Cascade rivers, pools separate stretches of fast rock-strewn rapids.

Your Action: ► Pools are usually excellent places for anadromous fish to rest up before tackling the next rapid. Trout will often set up housekeeping there as well.

Home free in the pool below boulder garden on the upper Clackamas River.

◄ **Pour-Over Rock:** Often preceding a hole or reversal, pour-overs are generally a noticeable drop over a fair-sized rock with a good flow of water. Sometimes these are found in the midst of a rapid and sometimes they are the only hazard on an otherwise friendly stretch of river. Sometimes they are followed by a reversal.

Your Action: ► Scout pour-overs before running them. It is not uncommon to find a rock spur that is invisible from above, but capable of ripping even stout aluminum boats. It is so much better to find something like that than to have it find you.

◄ **Rapid:** A definable section of river usually marked by an obvious drop, turbulent white water, and standing waves, or sometimes by a fairly benign drop followed by standing tail waves. Often a dangerous section of river, rapids can be filled with hazards and obstacles like rocks, logs, holes, and strainers. They can be a lot of fun to run. You had best know what you are doing if you are in a driftboat in a rapid. (See "Holes" and "Strainers").

Your Action: ► Predetermine a route that will guide you safely through and around obstacles and hazards in the rapid. If you cannot see it well from your boat or if it appears to be big (Class III or more), scout it from below.

◄ **Reversal:** Also known as: holes, keepers, white eddies, etc. A river feature that occurs after a sudden drop over a rock, ledge, or even a tree. As the falling water, its speed increased by the drop, meets the slower water below, a wave is created that breaks back over itself. This creates an upstream or reverse flow of water. Reversals can be sized from so tiny as to be barely noticeable with no effect on a boat to giants that can flip a boat as though it were a child's toy in a bathtub. (See "Holes," "Keepers," and "White Eddies.")

Diagram of the dynamics of the current flow through a reversal.

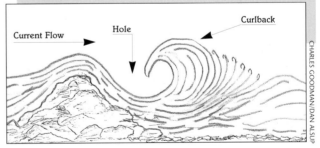

Your Action: ► Small ones can be ignored unless there is a submerged boulder that could hang you up. Reversals below large exposed rocks are white eddies which can be great places to rest or fish. Very large reversals such as at Martin's Creek rapid on the McKenzie River, are dangerous and sink several driftboats every year. Avoid them. Set up early with a well-thought-out route, perhaps one that you have watched someone else run successfully, and avoid the trouble spots.

Classic reversal. This one is in Martin's Creek rapid on the McKenzie River. It sinks dozens of driftboats each year, but it is not hard to avoid if you start setting up early enough.

The two photos below are both of the same piece of water. As you can see, the view from a boat upstream of the rapid is completely different from what is seen at a distance.

A typical riffle. Shallow technical water that requires simple maneuvering to stay off the gravel. This particular riffle on the Clackamas has some very productive pocket water.

CAROL DOWELL

◄ **Riffle:** A rapid too small to be rated. Riffles usually are very shallow with small choppy waves over gravel bottoms. Careful planning and judgment in choosing where the deepest channel lays will save you some time dragging and pulling your boat back into water deep enough to float it.

◄ **River Velocity:** The speed of the current. The average speed of the current in rivers is about 5 MPH or less but speeds of 10 MPH or so can be achieved through a rapid.

◄ **Rock Garden:** A section of river choked with rocks, usually smaller than those found in a boulder garden, but otherwise the same.

▶ *Your Action:* Rock gardens require precise rowing and water reading to get through without hanging up or capsizing. You must be confident and at ease on the oars and your rowing actions must come without mechanical thought. (See "Boulder Garden" page 49).

◄ **Roller:** This term usually refers to a large standing wave which is breaking back on itself like an ocean breaker or roller. Sometimes it refers to a large wave in a reversal. (See "Curler" and "Standing Wave").

◄ **Rooster Tail:** A rooster tail is first visible as a near vertical plume of water that seems to shoot skyward off a rock. Actually they are usually caused by the splash of a curler in a hole. Rooster tails are sometimes your first visual indication of an upcoming rapid. As you move closer to the entrance to a rapid, the less obvious they become.

◄ **Sidecurler:** A curler that is somewhat parallel to the current, these are usually found along irregular cliffs and shoreline rocks in heavy water. Also found on tight or fast outside corners. Also called laterals.

▶ *Your Action:* These can be tricky. In a narrow channel, with large standing waves in mid channel, side curlers can be nasty.

◄ **Sleeper:** A submerged boulder that is unmarked by ripple or wave, but is shallow enough to give you some kind of trouble if you hit it. In very fast water, collision with a sleeper could possibly cause you to capsize.

▶ *Your Action:* Learn the location of sleepers by memorizing the river at low flows. Listen to others whom are more familiar with the water than you and when on the water keep a sharp eye. Usually, if you are alert you will spot them.

◀ **Souse Hole:** Souse holes are smaller reversals. These mini-hydraulics can be strong enough to grab your boat and slow your momentum.

Your Action: You should be able to push through it even if it grabs you for a moment.

in Chapter Five were strainers and almost the scene of a disaster.

Your Action: Strainers are obstacles that should be totally avoided. When they block an entire channel they must be lined or portaged.

Standing waves on the lower Clackamas River.

◀ **Standing Waves:** Large waves that are created by a collision of fast water meeting slower water. Sometimes these waves appear, inexplicably to the eye, in the middle of a stream. Most of the time though, you will find standing waves in the tail end section of a rapid. Here they joyfully dance and frolic while beckoning you to go for a ride. These tailout waves usually offer exciting river roller coaster rides. (See "Tail Waves".)

Your Action: While they can be fun, approach them with care and caution. Big ones can drench your passengers and even precipitate a tip over.

◀ **Stopper:** A stopper is a reversal large enough to stop your forward momentum and require you to row downstream with some power.

With an intense look of concentration, Prince Helfrich slides over a log in the debris-choked Metolius River in about 1939. It is not uncommon to find debris like this, or worse. Inquire and scout.

This snag is a nasty root wad below the surface, a potentially lethal strainer.

◀ **Strainers:** Strainers are one of the most dangerous obstacles on the river. Often strainers look innocent to the untrained eye. This kind of obstacle allows the passage of water, but not objects or people. Strainers are often lethal when they combine with strong currents to catch an unlucky swimmer or boat. The trees described

◀ **Tail Waves:** A row of standing waves found at the end of a rapid when it meets slower waters or empties into a pool. (See "Standing Waves.")

Tail waves at bottom of Martin's Creek Rapid.

◄ **Technical Water:** Water that is strewn with in-stream boulders and other obstacles that require you to make many course changes in order to negotiate. Martin's Creek Rapid on the McKenzie River is considered to be technical water, in fact, the whole upper McKenzie is, as is Blossom Bar Rapid on the Rogue and the whole upper Clackamas River.

Oarsmen negotiating some very technical water on the Middle Fork of the Salmon in Idaho. (Kenny King in the front boat and Kenny Taylor in the rear boat.)

COURTESY OF KENNY KING

Your Action: This kind of water can be very fishable and is the kind of water that will turn you into a great boatman if you will let it.

Tongue or v slick entry to a rapid.

◄ **Tongue:** A "V" that points downstream. Smoother and darker than the surrounding white water, tongues often mark the safest entry to a rapid.

◄ **V Slick:** A tongue marking a downstream channel when pointing downstream. The marker of a rock or other obstacle when pointing upstream.

Driftboat entering a rapid on the tongue, the narrow band of dark water in front of the boat.

◄ **White Eddy:** An aerated (whitewater) eddy usually found downstream from an above-surface obstacle.

White eddy behind a large rock. When the water fills in behind downstream side of a rock, an upstream flow is created (an eddy). When the flow is fast, the water becomes aerated which makes it frothy and white. A boat can be parked in behind the downstream side of a rock to rest or fish. It will be held there by the upstream flow of the eddy and kept off the rock by the resulting cushion of water rolling back off the rock.

White Eddy

Difficulty and Danger Ratings of Rapids

In order to help newcomers and sojourners plan a drift and correctly evaluate the difficulty of a piece of water prior to running it, two systems of classifying rapids have been developed.

Rivers and rapids are generally classed according to their levels of difficulty or danger. Many have different classifications that are determined at different river flows. Some become extremely dangerous at higher flows. Others fill in and become flat water above a certain level. Conversely, there are rapids that as the water level drops, become tricky and even life-threatening. This knowledge is important because not all guide books or logs are able to give a complete description of all rapids at all flow levels. Unless you are willing to risk your boat and maybe your life, it is recommended that before you run new water on your own, you invest some time and money with a boatman experienced with the river and the flow you wish to run. Discuss the river and ride with or follow him down it. See how this river works and see how the locals do it. You might even learn some secrets about fishing in their neck of the woods.

If you choose to run a new piece of water on your own the first time, still take time to read a river log and compare notes with someone already experienced with that river. After that, use good common sense and scout what you can't see your way through. You should scout all rapids that are Class III or higher and if you can't see through it. **Scout it if it is Class III or more.**

Two scales are used to classify rivers and rapids as to both difficulty and danger. The most common scale in use is the International Scale, while the other scale is known as the Western Scale. The Western Scale utilizes more numbers (1-10) than the International Scale which only uses (1-6), which are often given a "+" to indicate increased difficulty or danger. The chart on this page is based on charts published by William McGinnis and R.W. Miskimins.

Mark Angel, a colorful local legend in the Deschutes River country of Central Oregon, successfully ran Sherars Falls, a very nasty Class VI on the Deschutes River, in a driftboat. He first ran it in a rubber raft. After spending his life on the river as a salvage expert, Mark has developed a very fine-tuned river sense. He has a unique understanding and perspective of the river's power and what its effects are on a boat. Please do not try this one unless you have had a lot of time on the river and know ahead of time exactly what is going to happen to you and your boat when you go over the big drop. Stay away from Sherars Falls. It is a Class VI rapid and can only be run at great risk of injury or even death.

These pictures below show the power and destructive abilities of fast water.

Scales of Difficulty

International			Western
Class	Skill Level	Description	Class
Un-classed	Beginner	Flat water, no rapids.	practice
I	Beginner	Very easy rapids, small waves, and only minor obstacles, that are easy to avoid, easy to read and find the route.	I-II
II	Novice	Bigger waves, experience and somemaneuvering required. Passages generally clear and there are no dangerous obstacles.	III-IV
III	Inter-mediate	Much more difficult. Irregular currents, rocks and eddies, course lines a little more difficult to define. Requires some experience reading water and skill on the oars and maneuvering under pressure. Dangerous obstacles and larger waves may be present, but can avoided only with moderate skill. Scouting is a real good idea.	V-VI
IV	Advanced	Requires a high degree of skill, difficult rapids with much chance of mishap. Requires precise maneuvering around dangerous holes, rocks etc. In very strong currents and turbulence. should be scouted before every run.	VII-VIII
V	Expert	Extremely difficult rapid requiring an extremely high degree of skill even in a raft. There are very few driftboaters crazy enough to attempt water this extreme. Rapids of this class are long with big drops, many obstructions, obstacles and violent hydraulics.	IX-X
VI	Crazy	There are some who will run the un-runable at a high risk of losing their lives.	U

Salvage expert Mark Angel pulls a driftboat up from the depths of the Deschutes River.

Sherars Falls on the lower Deschutes River. Named after an early settler, Sherars is a nasty near-vertical drop into a narrow chasm of frothy, aerated white water that can barely support the weight of a boat. Only one man has been known to run this in a driftboat; he does not encourage a repeat performance of this feat.

Drifting A River

Planning Your Drift

When you venture out on a river you enter a hostile environment. Extra care and vigilance are required if you plan to avoid disaster or tragedy. Every trip should be viewed as an adventure, a risky undertaking not to be taken lightly. Eagerness and enthusiasm must be tempered by prudence and forethought. No one plans a disaster, but many fail to plan.

Every time you entertain the notion of running a river, be it a placid piece of frog water or a raging whitewater torrent, ask yourself, "The lives of my companions and myself are worth a few extra minutes, aren't they?" If you answer yes, then take just a few minutes and go through a checklist to ensure that you have thought ahead, looking out for their safety and your own. Everybody is worth it!

Veltie Pruitt and Prince Helfrich often stacked their boats for economy when transporting them any distance. In this late 30s/early 40s photo, their friend 'Irish' poses at the summit of McKenzie Pass. Mt. Washington and Belknap Crater are in the background.

COURTESY OF ROY PRUITT

Be Prepared For Emergencies—Before Your Float

Have the proper safety gear for your activity and know how to use it. Swiftwater rescue courses are an excellent way to make sure that in a pinch, you have been trained, are up to date in your knowledge. Carry a good first-aid kit with fresh supplies. Update your training and proficiency in first aid and CPR. If you are not up to date, call your local Red Cross for a schedule of times, locations, and fees. It takes eight hours to complete a course and you need to update it every two years. See Chapter 11 for a checklist of first-aid supplies.

Make sure you are prepared when an emergency happens. Practice your emergency skills. Have contests with your friends throwing a rescue rope at a target or to people in a lake, pool, or stream. Review your first-aid techniques from time to time. Check your gear and supplies regularly. Work on your physical conditioning. You do not want to have a heart attack when you're having a good time or if you are needed to rescue someone else. Practice swimming, both in rapids and flat water. A little effort goes a long way towards preparation.

Know Your Passengers' Abilities and Limitations

Take the time to inquire of your passengers about any medical conditions that anyone might have. It is a good idea to find out about food allergies or any other special dietary needs they may have. Make sure that you get this information early in the planning process in order to properly prepare for a safe and enjoyable time for all members of your group.

Know Your Abilities and Limitations

Do not tackle water for which you are not prepared. If you have doubts about your ability to run a section of white water, then do not subject your guests or yourself to the unnecessary risk. Line around water where you do not feel confident, or water you know to be overly dangerous.

Use Checklists to be Sure You Have All the Necessary Gear

You want to be the kind of riverman who is prepared both with the proper equipment and with the knowledge of how to use it. Taking the time to do a checklist will certainly go a long way toward making sure you are fully prepared. If an airline pilot didn't bother with a pre-flight checklist and a tragedy occurred, and he survived, he could be held criminally negligent. We have all forgotten something at one time or another. That's why we need the checklist.

If you want to fish for steelhead you'd best bring your rain gear. Using a checklist is a good way to ensure that nothing is left at home.

Perform a Pre-Trip Check Before You Leave Home

Create a simple checklist which will help make sure you are leaving home with all the gear you will need. At o'dark-thirty in the morning, before you have gotten rid of all the cobwebs in your head, it's hard enough to remember your own name let alone to put the net in the boat. Using a checklist could turn out to be a real image saver with your friends and guests. See Chapter Eleven for a pre-launch checklist.

File a Float Plan

This is a simple itinerary that you leave with friends or authorities so that in an emergency situation you, and someone at home, can be located. If you are late coming off the river because you have run into problems, help will have a clue as to where to look for you. This can be a lifesaver if someone is in need of emergency medical aid or rescue. There should be no shame in a rescue party finding you OK, just delayed. Rescue parties tend to prefer finding the objects of their search alive and well. (Having to be rescued when you don't need to be too often would, of course, be an awfully good reason to reevaluate your skills and judgment.) A float plan does make the rescue job a little easier, which means quicker rescue help to you.

Teach Proper Techniques to Your Guests

Have a safety drill prior to each float. Use the checklist to make sure you cover all applicable points and then give a copy of the checklist to each of your guests. Remember: It is your boat, you are the skipper. You are responsible for the safety of your passengers, you have the right and the obligation to insist on following safe procedures.

Drifting a River—Trim Your Load

Balance your load so that you are not listing or leaning to one side or the other. Your boat will ride and row much better if it is loaded evenly, side to side, front to back. It is helpful to have the bow slightly heavier than the stern.

Save Alcoholic Beverages Until After the Float Is Over

Alcohol in your system clouds your judgment and will reduce your body's ability to keep itself warm. On the river you need a clear mind to best judge the ever-changing situation and to react correctly to whatever emergency comes up. Alcohol will also reduce your chance of survival in cold water because of how it affects your circulatory system, making it harder for your body to warm itself. Alcohol accelerates the onset of hypothermia. It will *not* make your day better or happier. There are healthier beverages to drink that won't ruin *anyone's* day.

Glen Wooldridge put it quite well to Florence Arman who related the following quote in her book *The Rogue: A River to Run*:

"One of the worst things you can do while running the river is to drink. I always hated that. It seems to me people shouldn't dim their minds with that stuff when there is so much on the river to see. It seems like it takes away the enjoyment. There's enough excitement just running rivers. That's the way I always felt about it."

Pay Attention, Keep Your Concentration (accidents happen instantly)

During the fall of 1991, Craig Lynch did a study of drift-boat accidents. These accidents had some common elements:
•All occurred in relatively easy water.
•All occurred due to operator error: hitting an object, fixed or floating.
•Accidents with driftboats happen very quickly with little or no warning.
The conclusion of this study seems to be:
1. Oarsman cannot let their guard down. Even easy water that appears to be benign can be dangerous and requires them to maintain their vigilance
2. PFDs in the box or stored under the front deck are useless. If a mishap occurs, most likely there will be no time to find and put on a PFD properly.

It would seem that proper precautions require constant vigilance and the wearing of life jackets (PFDs). As the reason for being on the river is primarily enjoyment, taking these precautions is merely a means toward the end you are seeking.

Marijuana Can Make Concentration Difficult and Definitely Alters Your Mental State

Pot just doesn't belong on the river. Moments of forgetfulness, "Hey man, I forgot where we were," just above Sherars Falls does not cut it! Our rivers are so awesome; there is so much beauty there. Why anyone would want to cloud it up with alcohol or drugs is way beyond me. Remember, you are responsible for the lives of your passengers—morally and legally—and that means financially. You are also responsible for anyone else injured by your carelessness on the water.

Keep Drugs Off the River!

Even in tiny doses, most drugs change your mental perception to some degree. In an emergency, would you want your life in the hands of someone who has been drinking or drugging? Wouldn't you want someone who is drug/alcohol free? When a passenger or guest has to depend on you, their life is in your hands. They expect that alcohol or drugs are not clouding your judgment and decisions.

Use Proper Sanitation Methods

Check the regulations in effect for the river you are going to float on, ignorance of the law will not work as a defense. Because so many people are using our rivers these days, it is becoming more and more important to clean up after ourselves. If we do not, we will be giving the Feds more reason (excuses) to take away some of our access to rivers and other public recreation resources. We need to pay more attention to correct disposal of our trash and human waste.

Trash Disposal

Carry a couple of garbage bags in your boat so you can pack out all of your own garbage. It doesn't hurt to pick up after some of the irresponsible folks as well.

Human Waste Disposal

Human waste disposal plans are in effect for almost every river system in the West. It is your duty to check with the authorities governing the management plan for the river you plan to float to determine which methods of disposal are required. The following methods demonstrate some of the various rules and methods for human waste disposal:

Liquid Waste

1. Urinate well above the high-water mark.
2. Urinate on the wet sand below a camp.
3. Dilution is the solution. Use a container and dump it in the fastest current.

Solid Waste

1. Carry a small trowel and bury your scat, again, well above the high-water mark. Biodegradable toilet paper can be buried but colored paper and other soiled personal items should be packed out. Carry small paper bags for this and put them into your big garbage bag after use.
2. Regulations are in effect on many rivers requiring you to pack out your solid waste. There are products on the market to help you with this. There are several portable toilets and container systems available to help you manage your pack-it-out requirements. Check the requirements of the managing authority for your river of choice and then check with your local outdoor sporting goods stores for more information on these products.

Carry Water or a Filter Device; Don't Drink River Water

Protozoa and parasites contaminate most of the pristine rivers in the great Northwest. These bugs can cause a lot of discomfort. To prevent this kind of problem, you must purify your water. There are three methods that are effective to varying degrees:

1. Boiling is the most effective method. Most of the little beasties are dead long before the water even boils. Boiling for 1 to 5 minutes is good insurance.
2. Chemical Treatment:
   A. Chlorine found in bleach is very effective. One capful in five gallons of water will do the job. The drawback is that it doesn't taste good unless you take the time to let the water stand for a couple of hours to give the chlorine a chance to evaporate.
   B. Iodine is an effective treatment against most, but not all, of the nasty river bugs. It will not kill Cryptospordium and can take up to an hour to kill *Giardia*. *Warning:* Many people are allergic to iodine.
   C. Filtering devices do an excellent job of removing impurities, contaminants, and river bugs.

Veltie Pruitt and George Godfrey take on some pretty hairy white water on the lower Deschutes in 1938.

I recommend using the filters for small amounts of water needed in a hurry and boiling for larger volumes.

With Regards to Rough Water and Obstacles, Set Up Well Ahead of Time

Maneuvering/rowing in rough water becomes much more difficult. You must make most course corrections by backferrying (angling the boat across the current pointing at where you don't want to be and rowing backwards). Put yourself in the best position to start your backferry as soon as is possible in order to build up your momentum so that you can easily have enough time and speed to hit your mark. Be very careful with your ferry angle. You do not want to be caught sideways in big waves or in deep troughs. In a tight situation, you will need to use that adrenaline-inspired strength to give you the extra boost needed for pulling with power on those oars. Do not dip your oar blades too deeply, no deeper than the point where the blade meets the oar shaft. You also want to time your strokes with the waves so that you are pulling against water and not flailing air. Usually this will be when you are on the wave and not in the trough. Turning in heavy water like this is easier on the wave as well. Remember to not let yourself get sideways to the waves in heavy water.

The Speed of the Current Will Usually Take You Through Big Waves

When faced with a big wave, it is a good idea to help out with some strong pushing. Give yourself additional momentum and power by rowing forward with all you've got into each wave.

Scout Big Rapids and All Rapids You Cannot See Through. Be Particularly Careful After a Flood and After Heavy Rains.

Logs, boats, and unknowns make it imperative that you scout a rapid if you cannot see all of it from top to bottom. Looking at a rapid from the downstream side up will show you where the rocks are much better than looking down will. Also, with every season, most floods, and even really heavy rains, the river will often change. Channels will be different, boulders and bars will move, and logs and debris will lodge in critical places and become strainers. You must exercise

Kenny King pushes his driftboat through Rubber Rapid—one of the toughest in a driftboat anywhere on Idaho's River of No Return.

extreme caution and be extra vigilant on even easy stretches of the river.

Guides lining their boats through Sulpher Falls, also known as Dagger Falls. This Middle Fork falls is just upstream of the current (1999) Middle Fork (of the Salmon River) put-in. Running the river above Dagger Falls is not commonplace since the new slide was installed.

COURTESY OF DAVE HELFRICH

Lining a Rapid

If you do not feel confident about running a section of river, line it. Every river-runner of note from John Wesley Powell to Prince Helfrich has lined one piece of water or another. Do not let your pride get in the way of going home safe at the end of a great river trip. Your loved ones will appreciate your coming home far more than hearing that you lost your life running the "big one."

Lining needs to be done with care. Sometimes lining a boat can be more dangerous than running a rapid. You can slip and injure yourself on the rocks quite easily. You could get yourself downstream of the boat and be squished between it and a rock. Even so, if you are not confident of making it through, by all means line it. Be extremely cautious. Wear your lifejacket and sandals or boots with felt soles or corkers as insurance against slipping. Use plenty of rope, bow and stern, to play the boat if necessary, but keep the unused portion coiled so no one gets tangled and accidentally pulled in. Watch out for quicksand and deep holes. Be unhurried and deliberate in taking your steps.

If in Doubt, Line Your Boat

Why take a chance with your boat, gear, and especially the lives of your passengers or yourself? If you are not sure, use extreme care and go around water that you do not feel good about. There is no shame in bringing everyone home safe and sound. I once lined an easy Class II rapid. My party and I were caught out late on a fall evening, I was not confident of my ability to safely run this particular rapid at night. My passengers were willing to run it and my river-wise friends told me

later that they believed I could have made it, but it was my call. We came home with the boat in one piece and all of our gear. More important, we came home alive with no injuries.

Once again, in *The Rogue: A River to Run* Glen Wooldridge gives us this sound advice:

"My theory of white water river running has always been proper equipment, properly used, and a healthy respect for the river."

"Of course, you aren't going to learn to swim until you get your feet wet, and it's the same with boating. But I don't advise beginners to start with the worst water they can find. "

"But I'm not trying to scare anyone off, either. I have had over sixty-five years of white-water running, and I wouldn't have missed it for the world.

"Driftboating is becoming popular on many of the rivers, nowadays. If you are thinking of drifting, I would suggest you make your first trip with a good river guide. That way you will have a chance to see the river and also how it is done.

"A good sound driftboat, at least 15 feet long, with a 4 1/2 foot bottom and a six foot beam is the best choice. You'll need three good 8 1/2 to 9 foot oars. Be sure to carry that extra oar; you never know when you will break one or lose one overboard.

"Oarlocks should be fastened in the sockets so they can't bounce out while you are rowing. That's what happened to us on the drift trip on the Salmon. The oarlock sprung and jerked the oar right out of Bruce's hand. Also, be sure the oars fit the oarlocks.

"For lining a boat, and just general safety, you'll need a fifty-foot bowline, or rope. You don't want to ever use a chain for an anchor line; sometimes you need to cut it quick, if you get hung up in swift water."

"Everyone in the boat should wear a life vest. A person hasn't got a chance if they are thrown out of a boat into the Rogue's rough waters without one. Their chances aren't too good, even with one. That old river has taken a lot of lives, just since I have been on it. You oughtn't to overload a boat, either. Three adults are just about all that can ride safely in a driftboat."

"You have to always keep your eyes open for trouble. It takes just about all your attention to run the river safely. Reading the water comes by experience. In whitewater every motion on top of the water is caused by something on the bottom. You have to learn what each rooster-tail of whitewater means. You learn where the boulders are and just how they are situated on the bottom by what is happening on top."

Rivers are wild creatures and even the most innocent in appearance is willing to claim your life in an instant. The rough waters of the Rogue River are not the only dangerous waters in the Pacific Northwest or elsewhere for that matter, and Glen's advice fits all waters. Safe boating practices should be followed way beyond the letter of the law—especially when operating driftboats on the rough waters of the Pacific Northwest.

Anchor With Care

When anchoring in midstream, some consideration must be given to the strength of the current. If it is way too strong your boat will sway back and forth wildly. This can be a minor inconvenience or a dangerous situation. If the boat is just mildly swaying back and forth, a sea anchor off the bow (or whichever end you have downstream) will hold you steady.

Note: There are two things to avoid when anchoring:

1. Avoid using a chain, you cannot cut it quickly enough.

2. Avoid anchoring over the side unless you want to see if you can roll your boat back up before it sinks.

Anchoring in big rivers with deep, strong currents can be very hazardous and has been known to sink boats. This kind of water requires rope at least three times longer than the depth of the water from boat to anchor. In addition to being three times the water depth your anchor rope should be 25 to 30% longer to ensure you have enough. You should be anchored from the bow to help prevent accidental swamping.

Always keep a sharp knife handy in case you must cut your anchor loose. You want your rope to be knot- and tangle-free in case of accidental anchor release. When drifting, it is not a bad idea to secure your anchor line to prevent accidental release. If you should drop your anchor accidentally in swift water and it hangs up, your boat could take a quick trip to the bottom. This has been known to happen when the transom has been pulled under. I can remember one incident in which a transom was pulled clean off the boat. If the knife is handy, you should be able to cut the line before you sink. Tying off your anchor to prevent accidental release is not a bad idea, but it is a hassle.

Driftboats, fish, and friends.

Protect Your Oars

Whether you are fishing with your boat at anchor, or lazily drifting with a slow current through frog water, ship your oars. That is, pull them up out of the water

Fishing below the high clay banks of the Clackamas.

and secure them. An oar suddenly getting stuck on the bottom could conceivably tip you right on over. The oar could also be pushed violently into you or one of your guests forcing someone overboard or causing serious injury. Besides that, you want those oar blades to last a while and not get all chewed up.

Check Your Oarlocks

Make sure that your oarlocks are bent together at the top just enough to firmly hold the oar in, but not so tightly that the oar shaft (not rope wrap) could not be popped in or out if put under some good pressure.

Stow Your Ropes Away

Should an accident occur, nobody needs to be getting tangled up in a loose rope. In fact, a loose rope could be the cause of an accident. I carry my extra rope in a bag or stow it in a dry box.

River Courtesy

When fishing and moving around other boats, please be thoughtful and respect their elbowroom and lines in the water. If someone is back bouncing or plugging down a drift, don't go for an end run and jump in front of them. Conversely, if you are plugging down a drift and you come up against some guys fishing off the bank, pull your lines and scoot by them as unobtrusively as possible. You can even ask if they prefer you passed by the close or far side. If someone is fishing in

the middle of the river, try to pass behind that person. Encourage friendliness and cooperation on the river.

Your goal should be to have an enjoyable day on the river, follow the rules and regulations that are in force and encourage others to respect and care for the resource, deal successfully with emergencies, and enjoy the safe return of yourself and your friends.

Privatization

The public, our rivers, and other publicly owned recreational areas are under siege today by forces that would have us surrender our rights to the use and enjoyment of our natural surroundings. Use of these areas is a birth right as well as tradition that dates back to before the founding of our country. These forces are fueled by big money and sneak up on us under the guise of conservation, environmentalism, and the euphemism "protect the resource."

Most of us are dedicated to preserving our wild lands, plants, animals, and rivers. Of course we want to contribute to a healthy environment, good management practices, and the preservation of our plants and wild life. Recreational users should not be blamed for all the damage to our environment, but they are! Major damage has occurred from logging, dams, and road building, but the government focuses on the recreational user rather than the real culprits.

The governmental fix is to limit our access through severe restrictions on use, access fees, etc. Fix what is easy and leave the tough calls for someone else to deal with. For example: There are way too many seals and sealions killing (not eating) our salmon and steelhead at a time when they are endangered. The correct solution would be to harvest enough seals and sealions so that a better balance could be achieved. Of course they will have to fight with Greenpeace and other misguided environmentalist types who do not understand that the balance of nature is out of whack. Seals and sealions have only two natural enemies left (in the lower 48 states)—killer whales and fishermen. When the protectors of the pinnipods used boats to run off the killer whales and laws to run off the fisherman, the pinniped populations exploded. They need to be harvested down to manageable levels. It is far easier, however, to leave the pinnipeds to their carnage (Jacques Cousteau calls them killers) and go after the recreational fishermen by restricting fishing through decreased bag limits and closures.

As time goes by, the recreational user and small-time guide will be forced completely out by closures and left at the mercy of giant corporate users. These corporate users will hold the use permits which you and I will need to be allowed back in—for a price. This process has already begun. Campground hosts employed by a big corporation back East now regulate our use at historically free or nominal-fee Forest Service campgrounds. If you wish to camp at a Forest Service campground, you must now make reservations with a private corporation in New York and pay a fee up front. You can forget that spontaneous weekend trip that you used to take when the weather suddenly turned nice.

Due to the demise of logging dollars and the lack of public resources to fund the big bureaucracies that are entrusted with our public lands, the bureaucrats are looking at big corporations as sources of operating capital. Big corporations are looking at public lands in terms of control and profit. You and I are asking that our taxes not be increased, so eventually we will be forced to pay a for-profit company to fish, boat, raft, camp, or hike. You will even need a permit to explore a cave. Of course, just as in the case of the Grand Canyon, you may be on a waiting list for years and pay a fortune for that very limited time/use permit.

Your contribution toward keeping our public lands and rivers free is needed. Become involved in local user organizations; encourage cooperation between different user groups. It will, of course, take more than a spirit of unity to save our heritage. We must actually work together or lose our rights. Practice responsible boating by following the laws and regulations that apply, being courteous towards all other river-users and practice pack-it-out. Quoting a sign posted by the present owners on Zane Grey's cabin on Winkle Bar, "Take only photos and leave only footprints."

Saturday morning driftboats at the put-in. Hendricks wayside on the McKenzie River, May 1999.

CHAPTER 10

Trouble on the River

IF YOU GET INTO TROUBLE, IT IS IMPORTANT THAT you maintain a level head. Do not quit, but rather increase your efforts and more than likely, with sheer faith and determination, you will pull yourself out of danger.

The ability to meet the challenges presented by adversity and prevail is prefaced by preparation. Are you prepared to meet the challenges of an emergency when on the river and in the wilds? You may have to save someone's life, perhaps your own. Will you be ready?

The following pages will show you what you can do to prepare, but they are only designed to let you know what is needed to prepare. You owe it to yourself, your passengers, and your fellow boaters to actually take the steps to get ready and be prepared to act.

Things Can Go Wrong

You are immersed in a hostile environment whenever you go drifting down a river. Nature will always be trying to throw you a curve. The more you learn, the more experience you gain, the more you will fit into this beautiful, wild, and hostile surrounding. The river will still try to claim you. You can be bruised, cut, suffer from hypothermia, or drown. When on the shoreline, you can fall, receive bruises, turned ankles, cuts and scrapes, stings from poisonous insects, and snakebites.

Driftboats enter Impassable Canyon on Idaho's river of No Return.

COURTESY OF KENNY KING

River warning sign located at entrance to the boat ramp at McIver Park on the Clackamas River.

There are even hostile plants that can make your life quite miserable. I know a lady who went for a walk in the dark along the Rogue River to have a conversation with Mother Nature. The plant life paid her back. While I did not see the result, I can assure you that it was not a pretty sight.

I can tell you ways to avoid river calamities. You can have all the experience in the world and have studied river rescue techniques, first aid, and CPR, still mishaps will occur. We are human beings and some things are beyond our control, people get in a hurry. They get tired and then just a little careless. There is not one of us who has perfect judgment. Sometimes mishaps will happen to us because of

Mark Angel carefully resurrects a sunken wooden driftboat from its watery grave in the Deschutes, there was only minor damage and this boat lived to dance again.

MARK ANGEL

others (other driftboats, rafters, or people who are fishing from the banks). When a mishap occurs most of us are not programmed to sit idly by; we will want to do what we can to help. To be an effective and positive help during a rescue attempt, giving first aid or even pulling a boat off a broach requires that you have had some training. When things go wrong, as we know they will, we need a preplanned method of handling the situation. No one plans to fail, but sadly, many fail to plan.

An emergency procedure that is well thought out and meticulously planned must be in place *before* it is needed. This emergency plan requires someone who has been trained and is practiced in the needed emergency procedures in order to do the right thing at the right time. Training, education, and practice also go a long way toward preventing confusion and hysteria. When the conscious mind becomes confused and out of focus because of stress or trauma, the subconscious mind will usually take over and try to do something. If there is no plan or rehearsed solution, your mind may grasp at straws, it will have no frame of reference from which to build a solution. If a plan has been rehearsed enough, it will become ingrained in the subconscious mind. The reaction to the rehearsed situation will become automatic. The subconscious mind will carry out procedures for which it has trained and rehearsed.

To Illustrate This Point . . .

I was once thrown out of a raft into a giant hole in the middle of a Class IV rapid. I was flushed downstream a couple hundred feet before I popped up for a quick breath and a look-see. I was able to orientate myself, but almost immediately I found myself in extreme turbulence, floating through big aerated waves.

In 45-degree water, without a wetsuit, I started to become confused. I was fighting for breaths in the turbulent troughs while struggling to expel the water that kept getting in my nose and mouth. The river was trying to overwhelm and drown me, it kept dunking me as I passed through another hole and some really big standing waves. My arms seemed to be flailing wildly like I was in a panic. Maybe I was. I recall my mind saying and asking of my arms, "Your arms look so stupid. What in the world are you doing?" My arms answered very matter-of-factly, "We are swimming." My mind said, "Oh yeah, that's good, keep it up."

Clearly, you can see how my subconscious mind realized that I needed to swim myself out of the river and went to it. I had a pre-programmed plan that enabled me to survive. I had enough experience swimming and had been in enough tight situations requiring swimming for survival for my mind to recognize that swimming was the workable solution. My mind also recognized the danger of hypothermia and went into action to eliminate that threat by ordering my body to leave that environment as quickly as possible—the start-swimming command was automatic. No mental discussion was required. This was a response to the training I have had to recognize hypothermia and the dangers associated with it. However, had I spent more time swimming rapids, I may have been able to relax and more calmly let the current push me to the bank. Maybe I could have expended a lot less effort and drank a lot less parasite-infested water.

There are different manifestations of fear. One is a realization of the danger of death or injury. Another is a kind of hysteria that usually stems from not having a well-rehearsed plan. Hysterical fear deprives you of rational thought. Rational thought is what you need to survive. It requires a plan of action. A calm person may be able to develop a plan of action if he has time. The hysterical person will not. Having a prescribed course of action indelibly inscribed upon your subconscious mind will help you calmly attempt to carry out the plan. When an emergency strikes, there may be no time to plan. Will you be the person with a plan?

Read and re-read the following plans. Memorize them. Prepare the equipment and supplies and go over this material again and again. This will help you program your mind to react positively to an emergency. A positive reaction to any given situation is more likely to produce a positive outcome. Do not end your survival education with just this material. Take the time to become certified in First Aid and CPR. Learn swiftwater rescue techniques. Take the time to stay in good physical condition. Swimming is an excellent exercise that will help you prepare for emergencies by toning your body, fine-tuning your swimming skills, and increasing your comfort level in the water.

River Emergencies and Solutions

Grounding Your Boat

Everyone who operates a driftboat will run it aground, sometimes several times in one day if they are operating on a river that is at low summer flow. Most of these groundings are no big deal, you just have to get out and push and pull your boat over the shallow sand or gravel bar. But even here you must be extremely careful. Slippery rocks and unseen drop-offs can combine with swift currents to turn the chore of pushing or pulling a driftboat into a hazardous undertaking.

Quicksand

Many of our western rivers have sandbars that are made up of loose, deep sand supersaturated with water. This situation is often at its worst after a flood or very high water when river sands are shifted around in the current and dropped in new places and are not yet settled. The result is quicksand. A misstep in quicksand and you will find yourself stuck and sinking. In some places the quicksand is only a couple of feet deep. In others it may be several feet deep, even over your head. Quicksand can have the consistency of thick soupy mashed potatoes or be like thick sticky wet concrete. You cannot swim in it, but you can drown or suffocate in it. The consistency of the quicksand will determine the rate at which you will sink. Struggling against it will only make you sink faster, in fact you will be sucked under.

Should one of your party get stuck in the sand, encourage them to keep still while you pull them out. If possible use a log or the boat to provide a platform from which to work. Using a rope will usually require more than one person so if you are alone use a Z-drag system to double your pulling power.

Your boat is your best defense against the hazards of the river bottom. When you are dragging or pulling your grounded boat, hold onto the gunwale in such a way that if you step into a deep hole or lose your footing on slippery rocks, the boat will support you. Exercise extreme caution when walking on an unseen or sandy river bottom. Test your steps to determine the firmness of the sand. In strong currents you must be wary of getting on the downstream side of the boat. It could push you over and entrap or injure you. Try to keep the boat perpendicular to the current. If you must swing it in the current to get around a rock, make sure that you have both bow and stern lines long enough to manage it and that no one is in a dangerous position downstream of the hull. Think through each move that you make and carefully evaluate what effect the current will have for each movement of the boat.

A Perforated Boat

Punching a hole in your boat does not have to be the end of your adventure. Provided your boat doesn't sink before you get it to the bank, you can easily make temporary repairs and finish your trip.

One fast repair that has been tried and proven is the old duct tape trick. This repair takes only minutes and does not require much of a repair kit. Simply cover the hole, inside and out, with a duct tape patch. Experienced guides have used this method on many trips to make sure their boats could finish. Karen Bigler, who sometimes accompanies her husband guide Eric, related a time when an ugly 10-inch gash that was a whopping 5 inches wide was knocked in the side of their wooden boat in Rattlesnake Rapid on the Deschutes River. Careful application of many layers of

Deschutes River guide Eric Bigler repairs a wooden driftboat with duct tape to hold back the water of the Deschutes. This repair enabled the boat to float the last several miles to the take out.

KAREN BIGLER

duct tape made possible the safe completion of the several more miles to the mouth.

In making emergency repairs you are limited only by the materials at hand and your own imagination. Having a repair kit with you will help you be prepared to meet the challenge of a perforated boat.

Sometimes a simple temporary measure can be taken just to get you over to the bank. Some friends of mine, Art and Kathryn Isrealson, were going over Blossom Bar Rapid on the Rogue and had an encounter with the edge of Picket Fence (a nasty rock sieve responsible for the demise of many boats and some folks). Somehow or another a hole was punched near the bottom of the boat. Kathryn used common-sense-inspired quick thinking and stuck a seat cushion into the hole and braced it with her legs. They were able to safely finish negotiating the boulder garden before pulling out to actually make a temporary patch.

For a repair that should hold up for several days, pull your boat up on the bank and turn it so that you can get to the hole. Clean up any rough edges by scraping off splinters of wood or fiberglass. Straighten torn and jagged metal by hammering it flat. Make sure that the surrounding area is clean and dry. Use sandpaper to rough the adjacent surfaces so that caulking might better adhere.

Use a piece of sheet metal from your repair kit. (See Chapter 11 for a Repair Kit Checklist.) Cut it so that it is larger than the hole by at least 2 or 3 inches each way—be generous but not ridiculous. On the outside of the hull, spread the caulking around the hole in the boat much the same way you would spread rubber cement to patch an inner tube. Put on a healthy bead that is thick enough to have a small amount of excess squeeze out on the perimeter of your patch when you apply pressure. When you have it laid in place, use self tapping metal screws for an aluminum boat or wood screws for a wood or fiberglass boats from your repair kit and secure it to the hull. Put in enough screws to ensure a completely tight fit. Repeat this process on the interior of the hull. This simple repair should be effective until you can reach your take out and effect permanent repairs.

Entrapment

When dragging a boat over a rock garden of basketball-sized or larger rocks there is always the possibility of twisting an ankle or breaking a bone. If there is much current, you run the risk of getting a leg stuck and falling or being pushed over by the current. If the current holds you there you could be in serious risk of drowning. Once again, holding onto your boat and testing your footing is the best chance you've got. Extreme caution must be exercised. If you become entrapped, you will need the help of someone else to be rescued—self-rescue from entrapment is rare.

Rocky Collisions

Crashing your boat into a rock can be a very noisy inconvenience or the onset of a major catastrophe. It might just be another dent in your boat or another scratch in the paint job. Then again, if you hit a very small rock with the downstream side of the boat, just below the water line in very fast and shallow water, you could easily find yourself and your boat upside down and a stupid silly grin on your face. If you ground yourself on a large rock in deep water, your upstream side or end could be forced under water. Another nasty possibility is that a new drain hole could be installed in the side or bottom of your hull. Avoid hitting rocks like you would avoid the plague, it's never good.

We all know colliding with rocks should be avoided but if you can't avoid them, hit them bow first. Your bow is very strong and able to withstand quite a bit of punishment. Once you have hit, you may be able to back off if the current is not too strong, or you can cartwheel around the rock—a maneuver the old-timers call 'bowing out'. Cartwheeling in a driftboat can be a risky maneuver but it may be your only way out. Cartwheeling means to use a double oar turn to spin yourself around the obstacle and then spin again to regain your proper downstream attitude. If you are in heavy water and big waves, you may have to ride it out backwards rather than take the chance of being caught sideways in a trough. The next cresting wave could swamp you. You really must avoid banging into rocks with your boat.

Broaching

Getting hung up on an above-surface object in the river can be a problem. The river will want to pour over your upstream side which would lead to swamping or capsizing. Your initial reaction should be to 'jump to,' a rafter's term that refers to jumping to the high side of the boat. The idea here is to push the downstream side (the side against the obstacle) down using your weight so that the upstream side will be held up by the water that will now be able to flow under it. This will result in your craft floating off the obstacle rather than having the hydrodynamics of the river force the upstream side of the boat under water. "Jumping to" should give you the opportunity to back the boat off or cartwheel around the obstacle. You may have to hold in this position until help arrives. Perhaps you will have to get a rope to the bank in order to pull your boat off. In any case, remain calm and look for solutions. The incident described at the beginning of Chapter 5 is a classic broaching, and while filling your boat with water is not the prescribed remedy to get off a broach or out of a strainer, it would not be uncommon to ship (take water over the side) some water.

It sure helps to have all of the boat. Pat Eastveld found this remnant of an aluminum boat along the Deschutes River

One way to pull the boat off would be to rig a Z-drag (or a heavier block and tackle) pulling system and pull your boat back upstream from the obstacle. (Naturally heavier equipment like a block and tackle, come-along, or winch would be a superior choice provided you have room to pack all that stuff along in your boat). Once again, caution is the key word. Make sure that no one is in the way and in danger of being knocked over or pinned between the boat and a boulder because they are downstream of the boat.

Swimming a Rapid

There are many accomplished driftboaters who have never had the misfortune of taking an unplanned swim in a cold raging torrent. On the other hand, there are many driftboaters that have. It is important to note that an accident is not always a reflection of the oarsman's ability; oftentimes accidents are caused by circumstances beyond his control. A professional river guide I know was in a situation in heavy water carrying a "heavy" load of fishermen. One of them panicked at the pitching of the driftboat (which was still under control). He stood up, fell against the other passenger and over went the boat. You just cannot have 600 to 700 pounds piled up against one side of the boat. Had the passenger remained seated, the boat would have maintained its trim (or balance) and the professional guide and his boat would have come through just as well as they had on countless trips prior to this one.

Knowing that a tip-over can happen to any one at any time, you are better off being prepared, wearing your PFD, and knowing how to swim a rapid. Your life and the lives of your passengers may someday depend on it.

The basics of swimming a rapid:

1. Be wearing your properly fitted and fastened PFD before you get dumped in the drink. You will have no time once the action starts—it will be that sudden.
2. In our ruggedly beautiful and very cold rivers a sudden immersion into ice-cold water can result in a gasping reflex that may cause instant drowning. Your best defense is to know that this potential for instant drowning exists and remember it. You can control the gasping reflex if you try, just remember that your system will most likely gasp when it hits ice-cold water—don't let it. Hold your breath tightly.
3. In fast, shallow water, swim on your back with your feet up and pointing downstream to ward off rocks. If your feet are dragging on the bottom of the river you run the risk of getting them trapped

and then the heavy current can hold you so that you cannot free yourself (see "Entrapment"). Swimming on your back, against the current, will allow you to backferry around obstacles and help you find the bank or the safety of a rock that you can climb onto. Stay on your back as you swim through the rapid into deeper, calmer water and then begin to swim using your strongest strokes. Swim with the current, angling toward the closest bank. Get out of the water as quickly as possible even if it means climbing up on a midstream rock and waiting for help. In our cold Pacific Northwest rivers, hypothermia is always a concern. Immersion in cold water can bring it on faster than any other way.

4. When you are going through a series of waves, breathe in the troughs and hold your breath through the waves.

5. If you are caught in a hole (keeper, reversal, etc.) try to swim out of it either by : a.) Swimming out the side. This is not as hard as it sounds. b.) Diving under the curling action and getting into the downstream flow. Tucking yourself into a ball will help the current wash you out faster. If the reversal is too big and powerful and you have no outside chance for rescue, it may become necessary to remove your PFD to swim down and under the reversal action. Remove your PFD only as a last resort!

6. Use your whistle to alert others to your situation. Listen for a whistle from someone who may be trying to get your attention as they try to throw you a rope or some other device that will require your active participation.

7. If you are wearing rubber hip or chest waders be sure all interior straps and ties are left undone so that if you should fall in, and the boots fill with water, they will easily slip off. If you are wearing neoprene chest waders make sure you are wearing a snug elastic chest belt to inhibit the entry of cold river water. The air in them may help you keep your feet up and help you maintain your core body temperature a little longer.

Rescuing a Swimmer

Your options are:

1. Throw a flotation device to give the swimmer extra flotation so he can self-rescue.

2. Throw a rope, either a heaving coiled line or a bagged rescue line. If you miss the swimmer with a bagged rescue rope and need to try again, coil the rope. It is much faster to coil the line than to bag it—and at a time like this every second counts.

3. Use an oar to reach the swimmer and pull him in the boat.

4. Use your boat to get alongside the swimmer and help him into your boat. Much care must be taken here as a mistake could cause you to lose shape in a rapid and put your boat and yourself in jeopardy. If you are in really rough water that demands your full attention as the oarsman, you must leave it to your passengers to pull the swimmer into the boat. If you can assist by moving the boat into a better position, good deal. If the water is too heavy, it most likely will be better to ride out the rough water with the swimmer holding on than to risk yourself and/or your passengers.

5. Use the Strong Swimmer method of rescue. That means a person going overboard to assist someone swimming. This should only be attempted by a very strong swimmer trained in rescue swimming. this is the most dangerous method and should only be used as a last resort.

Important Note: If at all possible, keep your boat parallel to the current and bring the swimmer in over the side. If your boat is sideways to the current, do not bring the swimmer in on the upstream side!! If the water is obstacle-free, then move the victim to the downstream side to pull him into the boat. This is the only circumstance in which you should ever allow a swimmer on the downstream side of your boat.

Certain types of accidents and the resulting injuries are common in outdoor settings. On the river you are likely to come into contact with the following injuries and illnesses:

Abrasions; broken bones; bruises; cuts; drowning; epileptic seizure; heart-related illness; heat-related illness or injury; hypothermia; insect bite or stings; sunburn; twists and sprains; and snakebites. Be prepared for all of them.

As an outdoors person, more than likely you are going to encounter minor injuries requiring that you administer minor first aid. It is not unlikely that you will be called upon to help someone with a life-threatening condition. The knowledge and skill that you have taken the time to acquire may mean the difference between life and death. The life you save may be that of someone you love. This book is not about first aid so I am not going to teach First Aid here, but rather point you to the agencies, like the Red Cross, local fire departments, and community colleges, which have excellent classes to meet that need. Avail yourself of their programs, spend the time, gain the knowledge, and develop the skills.

Be one worthy to ride with on the river.

CHAPTER 11

Checklists For Driftboaters

Checklists

- Survival Kit Checklist
- First-Aid Kit Checklist
- Sanitation Kit Checklist
- Repair Kit Checklist
- Lunch Box Checklist
- Kitchen Box Checklist
- Camping Gear Checklist
- Individual's Checklist (Day Trip)
- Individual's Checklist (Multi-Day Trip)
- Float Plan
- Pre-Trip Checklist
- Passenger Safety Briefing
- Driftboat Checklist

Survival Kit Checklist

- Waterproof Matches
- Whistle
- Mirror
- Fire Starter
- Water Purification Tablets
- Minor First-Aid (Band Aids, aspirin, etc.)
- Hot Drink Mix
- Large Metal Cup (military canteen cup works well)
- Emergency Stove
- Emergency Fuel
- Rain Poncho
- Space Blanket
- High-Energy Bars
- Waterproof Pouch
- Knife
- Flashlight
- Compass
- 100 Feet of Parachute Cord
- Survival Booklet
- Map of the Area

First-Aid Checklist

Bandages

- ❏ 1" Bandages (10)
- ❏ Butterfly Strips
- ❏ Adhesive Tape
- ❏ Gauze Pads
- ❏ 4" X 4" (4)
- ❏ 2" X 2" (4)
- ❏ 2" Gauze Roll (1–2)
- ❏ Triangular Bandage
- ❏ Sanitary Napkins (2)
- ❏ Moleskin
- ❏ Tincture of Benzoin
- ❏ Wound-Closure Strips
- ❏ Elastic 'ace' Bandages

Pain Medications

- ❏ Aspirin (10)
- ❏ Acetaminophen (10)
- ❏ Ibuprophen (10)
- ❏ Analgesics (Ben Gay, etc.)
- ❏ Burn Gel
- ❏ Benadryl
- ❏ Aloe Vera Gel
- ❏ Hydrocortisone Cream
- ❏ Antacids
- ❏ Rehydration Salts
- ❏ Anti-Diarrheal
- ❏ Pepto Bismal/Alka Seltzer

Supplies

- ❏ Nitrile Glove
- ❏ Sam Splint
- ❏ Hypothermia Thermometer
- ❏ CPR Mask
- ❏ Snakebite Kit
- ❏ Emt Scissors
- ❏ Q-Tips
- ❏ Glucose Paste
- ❏ Safety Pins
- ❏ Duct Tape
- ❏ Pencil/Paper
- ❏ Extra Zip-lock Bags
- ❏ Forceps or Tweezers

Cleaning Items

- ❏ Surgical Scrub Brush
- ❏ Waterless Hand Cleaner
- ❏ Antiseptic Towlettes
- ❏ First-aid Pads (w/Lidocaine)
- ❏ Saline Solution
- ❏ Hydrogen Peroxide
- ❏ Providone Iodine Solution
- ❏ *Wilderness and Travel Medicine*, by Eric Weiss, MD. This first-aid book recommends antibiotics and pain medications that your doctor can prescribe for wilderness trips.

Pre-Trip Checklist

❏ Tire Check   ❏ Gasoline

❏ Trailer   ❏ Auto Lights

❏ Vehicle   ❏ Trailer Lights

❏ Spares   ❏ Float Plan

❏ Fluids Check   ❏ Driftboat List

❏ Brake Fluid   ❏ Fishing Gear

❏ Transmission Fluid   ❏ Maps

❏ Oil   ❏ Special Information (fishing reports,

❏ Extra Oil For Trip   phone numbers, etc.)

Additional Items

❏ _____   ❏ _____

❏ _____   ❏ _____

❏ _____   ❏ _____

❏ _____   ❏ _____

❏ _____   ❏ _____

Shuttle Arrangements

Shuttle Company:_____

Shuttle Specifics:_____

_____

_____

_____

Sanitation List

❏ Toilet Paper (In zip-lock bag)

❏ Hand Trowel

❏ Kitchen-Size Garbage Bags

❏ Small Plastic Bags (individual

   use for TP)

❏ Portable toilet and supplies if

   required. Check regulations for

   your river.

❏ Biodegradable Soap or Waterless

   Hand Cleaner

Additional Items

❏ _____

❏ _____

❏ _____

❏ _____

❏ _____

❏ _____

❏ _____

❏ _____

❏ _____

Break time on the Rogue River

COURTESY OF CLACKAMAS MARINE

Driftboat Checklist

❏ PFDs: One Type III or V for each

person on board, plus an extra.

One Type IV Throwable Per Boat

❏ Sanitation Kit

❏ 3 or 4 Oars

❏ Bailing Bucket (1-5 gallon)

❏ Anchor and Line Rope

❏ 100 feet of Extra Rope

❏ Repair Kit

❏ Survival Kit

❏ First-Aid Kit

❏ Cooler

❏ Lunch/Kitchen Box

❏ Food and Drink

❏ Water Supply

❏ Garbage Bags

❏ Personal Gear

❏ Fishing Gear (as per individuals'

checklists)

Optional Items

❏ _____

❏ _____

❏ _____

❏ _____

❏ _____

❏ _____

❏ _____

❏ _____

❏ _____

❏ _____

❏ _____

❏ _____

❏ _____

❏ _____

❏ _____

❏ _____

Repair-Kit Checklist

❑ Spare Oar Lock

❑ Spare Oar Stop

❑ Spare Plug

❑ Duct Tape

❑ 2-Foot-Square 26-Gauge Sheet Metal

❑ Caulking That Will Adhere to Wood

  or Metal

❑ Small Battery-Powered Drill

❑ Extra Charged Battery for Drill

❑ Drill and Screwdriver Bits

❑ 15 to 20 Self-Taping Sheet Metal

  Screws or Wood Screws 1/2 to 1" In

  Length

❑ Screwdrivers: One Phillips, One

  Slotted

❑ Hammer and/or Hatchet

❑ Locking Pliers or Clamps

❑ Small Saw

❑ Tin Snips and Adjustable Pliers

Additional Items

❑ _____

❑ _____

❑ _____

❑ _____

❑ _____

❑ _____

❑ _____

❑ _____

❑ _____

❑ _____

❑ _____

❑ _____

❑ _____

❑ _____

❑ _____

❑ _____

Camping Gear Checklist

❑ Tent

❑ Ground Tarp

❑ Rain Canopy

❑ Lanterns

❑ Fuel

❑ Fold-Up/Roll-Up Tables

❑ Camp Chairs/Stools

❑ Camp Cots

❑ Ax or Hatchet

❑ Fire Starter

Additional Optional Items

❑ _____

❑ _____

❑ _____

❑ _____

❑ _____

❑ _____

❑ _____

❑ _____

Individual's Checklist (Day Trip)

❑ Shoes or Waders

❑ Rain Gear

❑ Windbreaker

❑ Coat

❑ Gloves

❑ Sun Hat

❑ Warm Hat

❑ Bug Juice (Repellant)

❑ Lip Balm

❑ Sunblock

❑ Camera and Film

❑ Binoculars

❑ Sunglasses

❑ Fishing Gear

Additional Optional Items

❑ _____

❑ _____

❑ _____

❑ _____

❑ _____

Individual's Checklist (Multi-Day Trip)

Personal Clothing

- ❏ Shoes
- ❏ Socks
- ❏ T-Shirts
- ❏ Warm Shirts
- ❏ Shorts
- ❏ Underwear
- ❏ Long Underwear
- ❏ Rain Gear
- ❏ Boots
- ❏ Waders
- ❏ Windbreaker
- ❏ Coat
- ❏ Sun Hat
- ❏ Warm Hat
- ❏ Gloves

Bedding

- ❏ Sleeping Bag
- ❏ Pillow
- ❏ Air Mattress
- ❏ Camp Cot

Optional Personal Gear

- ❏ Camera and Film
- ❏ Binoculars
- ❏ Games (cards, chess, etc.)
- ❏ Sunglasses
- ❏ Musical Instrument
- ❏ Books
- ❏ Gold Pans, etc.
- ❏ Bug Repellant
- ❏ Fishing Rods and Reels
- ❏ Tackle and Bait

Optional Items

- ❏ _____
- ❏ _____
- ❏ _____
- ❏ _____
- ❏ _____
- ❏ _____
- ❏ _____
- ❏ _____
- ❏ _____

- ❏ _____
- ❏ _____
- ❏ _____
- ❏ _____
- ❏ _____
- ❏ _____
- ❏ _____
- ❏ _____
- ❏ _____

Lunchbox List

❑ Salt and Pepper

❑ Napkins

❑ Paper Plates

❑ Eating Utensils

❑ Plastic Cups

❑ Serving Utensils

❑ Biodegradable Soap or Waterless

   Hand Cleaner

❑ Tablecloth

❑ Roll-Up/Fold-Up Table and Chairs

Additional Items

❑ _____

❑ _____

❑ _____

❑ _____

❑ _____

❑ _____

❑ _____

❑ _____

❑ _____

❑ _____

Deschutes River camp.

ERIC BIGLER

Kitchen Box Checklist

- ❏ Water Purification System
- ❏ Tablecloth
- ❏ Napkins
- ❏ Cups and Plates
- ❏ Eating Utensils
- ❏ Kitchen Utensils and Knives
- ❏ Biodegradable Soap, for Dishes, Etc.
- ❏ Wash Basin, for Dishes or Sponge Baths
- ❏ Dish Cloths and Scrubbers
- ❏ Kitchen Towels and Paper Towels
- ❏ Waterless Hand Cleaner
- ❏ Salt and Pepper
- ❏ Sugar
- ❏ Flour
- ❏ Spices and Seasonings
- ❏ Coffee, Tea, Hot Chocolate, Etc.
- ❏ Aluminum Foil
- ❏ Plastic Wrap
- ❏ Wooden Strike-Anywhere Matches
- ❏ Bug Juice (Repellant)
- ❏ Camp Stove and Fuel
- ❏ Flashlights and Batteries
- ❏ 2 Frying Pans
- ❏ Sauce Pans
- ❏ Dutch Oven
- ❏ Two Kettles for Boiling Water
- ❏ Buckets for Washing Dishes, Carrying Water, Etc.
- ❏ Coffee Pot and Tea Kettle
- ❏ Clothes Line and Clothes Pins

Additional Items

- ❏ _____
- ❏ _____
- ❏ _____
- ❏ _____
- ❏ _____
- ❏ _____
- ❏ _____
- ❏ _____
- ❏ _____
- ❏ _____
- ❏ _____
- ❏ _____

- ❏ _____
- ❏ _____
- ❏ _____
- ❏ _____
- ❏ _____
- ❏ _____
- ❏ _____
- ❏ _____
- ❏ _____
- ❏ _____
- ❏ _____
- ❏ _____

▶

Float Plan

River: _____

Trip Leader: _____   Number In Party: _____

Put-In Date: _____   Put-In Location: _____

Take-Out Date: _____   Take-Out Location: _____

Take-Out Time: _____   ETA Home: _____

Phone Check-in Time:
_____

If check-in call not received by _____ (day) _____ (time), notify River Authority:

   Name: _____   Phone number: _____)

Emergency Numbers

Name	Contact	Phone Number
_____	_____	_____
_____	_____	_____
_____	_____	_____

Campsites

Night/1st Choice	Alternative (2)	Alternative (3)
1. _____		_____
2. _____		_____
3. _____		_____

Additional Information

_____

_____

_____

_____

_____

Passenger Safety Briefing

❏ PFDs: When To Wear Them _____ How To Fit Them _____

❏ If You Fall In: _____ Swimming a Rapid _____

❏ Jumping Highside _____

❏ Helping Someone Into the Boat _____

❏ Standing In Boat: When and When Not To _____

❏ Sanitation Procedures and Kit _____

❏ Rescue Ropes: Location _____

❏ Emergency Rescue Gear: Location _____

❏ First-Aid and Survival Kits: Location _____

❏ Description of Area and Emergency Instructions _____

❏ Rendezvous If Separated: How and Where _____

❏ Emergency Evacuation Plans _____

❏ Garbage/Waste Management _____

Wildlife

❏ Sightings _____

❏ Dangers (if any) _____

❏ Protective Measures (if called for) _____

Other Items of Localized Interest

_____

_____

_____

_____

_____

CHAPTER 12

Look to the Future

AT THE TIME OF THIS WRITING, ALMOST 200 YEARS of drifting our western rivers have passed. The first 100 years of river travel was almost entirely devoted to exploration and practical transportation. The second 100 years has seen most of the western rivers domesticated by commercial enterprise and heavy recreational use.

The mighty rivers of our country are now highways for tug and barge traffic and playgrounds for pleasure craft. The people of our nation have a love of the water.

Driftboats blend in with the multitudes fishing for spring chinook at Oregon City near the mouth of the Clackamas, May 1999.

We not only love the water, we have a particular affinity for spending time *on* it—some in the wide variety of sailing craft, others prefer motored pleasure boats, which come in all sizes and shapes. There is everything from tiny personal watercraft to fancy cigar boats and cabin cruisers to big, beautiful ocean-going yachts. Commercial vessels offer scenic tours on our big waterways in luxury liners and stern-wheeled steamers. Big jet boats offer a different kind of scenic tour on wild whitewater rivers. There are both private and commercial whitewater thrill-seekers to be found running the more wild and extreme white water in rafts, kayaks, and driftboats. The largest number of boats in this country are, however, fishing boats and the driftboat was designed for just that purpose.

Unfortunately, the proliferation of development and enterprise, the very things that have given our

Lori-Ann Murphy of Reel Women is an Idaho fishing guide.

COURTESY CLACKAMAS MARINE

nation its vitality and wealth, are taking a toll on our natural resources and the once-abundant fish are in short supply. Guides who have taken people fishing over the last 50 years complain there are "too many people and boats on the rivers, the true wilderness experience and the fish are getting scarce."

The next complaint of course is government regulation that stifles use and makes it tough for the little guy to make a living.

These problems have arisen from mismanagement by government agencies and too much greedy competition for limited resources. Our success at running businesses and exploiting the opportunities handed to us when we won this continent have left us a legacy of

Haldane 'Buzz' Holmstrom and his boat the *Silver Steak*. The full story of Buzz and his boat is told in the book, *The Doing Of The Thing*.

VINCE WELCH, BRAD DIMOCK, AND CORT CONLEY

Buzz Holmstrom and his boat, after 52 days of navigating 1100 miles and over 365 rapids of the Colorado River. The only man who ever conquered the Colorado alone. He arrived at Boulder dam Nov. 25, 1937

assorted environmental and resource management problems. While we are not in danger of losing the right to hunt and fish, we are losing our rights to hunting and fishing grounds, species, and the expectation of success. We are also facing battles to boat the rivers we wish to when we want to.

A 1998 book, *The Doing of the Thing*, tells the story of the brilliant whitewater career of Buzz Holmstrom. In 1937, Buzz decided that he was going to run the Green and Colorado rivers in a boat that he would build for himself. He built the boat and practiced on the Rogue, Umpqua, and Coquille for "doing his thing." He became the first person to solo through the Grand Canyon. You and I are not allowed to do that in as casual a manner today. We may spend several hundreds of dollars a day and pay a commercial outfitter to take us down the river, or we can take a number (for a fee) and wait in line for twelve to fifteen years to obtain a permit to run the river. The last alternative we may have would be to join or become an outfitter and have the opportunity to run the river a lot. These same kinds of restrictions are present on many of our rivers both in Oregon and elsewhere although the waiting lists are not as long anywhere else. Too many people and too few resources.

We cannot solely blame the big outfitters for the problems. They provide wild-river experiences for those among us who are unable to enjoy the experience otherwise. There are those who are more comfortable and secure in the hands of a professional who spends a lot of time on the river. Still a solution needs to be found for the controversy that exists between private boaters and outfitters over equitable distribution of the river trip permits. The number of private boaters is increasing at a tremendous rate. This is a big change from when the professionally operated boats were in a great majority. The result is private boaters are getting a smaller and smaller percentage of the permits allocated.

I've noticed that all of the rivers with controversy over permit distribution are rivers run by agencies of federal bureaucracies. Perhaps each state should take control of the beds and banks of the rivers. They are, after all, owned by the people of the states as granted by federal law governing navigability. Once the states have control they should be managed much as the beaches in Oregon are, as public highways, free to all. We don't close a highway just because its crowded do we? No! We manage it and police it.

The only alternative that is workable is for the federal agencies to turn to the public—whom they work for and for whose interests they are responsible—and, in a public forum, work to find answers that are satisfactory for all. It is up to us to demand accountability.

Accountability by government will only exist if we get involved and stay involved. It is our job to hold those who work for us accountable. If we do not do that, then we deserve the loss of our freedoms. Someday they will be like the salmon, severely wiped out and on the way to extinction.

Jim "Coz" Costolnick guides his clients to trophy trout along the Delaware River in New York State. Bob prefers a fiberglass driftboat.

COURTESY OF CLACKAMAS MARINE

Another great issue we face in Oregon and several other western states is navigability. Congress set aside the navigable rivers of the West as public highways just as the ocean beaches were. Our state government failed in the beginning to declare which rivers were going to be considered navigable. Since then it has sidestepped the issue because of the political quagmire dealing with it could bring. It was and is their job to clarify this issue. They shirked their duty and now we have a mess. Local landowners are stymied from prosecuting trespassers when trespassing occurs on land, which is considered public domain under federal statutes. River people are wary of getting themselves in a legal entanglement if they try to fight prosecution for violation of trespass laws not supported by State or Federal law. We need some legislators who are more interested in doing the right thing, meeting the issue head on and solving it rather than being more interested in their own political careers. This issue needs to be resolved soon and in a manner that is equitable for everyone.

We must also improve the way we manage ourselves. We must obey the rules and regulations that we (through our elected officials) set up. We must respect the rights of the property owners on whose lands we sojourn irrespective of current legal wrangling. The number one issue is leaving a mess and interfering with the landowner (leaving gates open, theft, and improper personal sanitation etc.). The number one enemy of the public in these issues is the public itself. At Winkle Bar on the Rogue River, the owners of the property adjacent to the river maintain a cabin once owned by Zane Grey, a prolific western writer of the early part of the 20th century. River travelers and sojourners stop and visit the site on a regular basis. The owners have put up a sign that reads, "Take Nothing But Photographs And Leave Nothing But Footprints." Luckily, most folks respect the rights of the owners and the site remains open. Hopefully, more river-users will be educated to be as respectful so that a peaceful co-existence based upon mutual respect between the river folk and landowners will prevail.

Bringing back the fish is a great challenge compounded by the lack of knowledge of how to accomplish it. Everyone has an idea, and the most knowledgeable, the trained biologists are frustrated by economic and political considerations. The answer lies with the people. If we are informed and want to accomplish the return of the great fisheries that we have known in the past, we must give a clear and uncertain mandate to our politicians that we will accept nothing less. The big question is, are we willing to pay the price, not only in dollars, but in lost jobs and in other changes in how we live our life. Our we willing to engage in catch-and-release-only fishing? Are we willing to give up destructive logging practices and gillnetting? We have the responsibility to ensure the treaty rights we promised the Native Americans and they have a responsibility to do their part in helping to restore the resource that is so central to their culture.

Unfortunately, the challenges we face on the river are exceeded by the challenges we must face in the legislature and in the halls of justice. If we desire to

This driftboat has been put out to pasture and has gone to pot. Not an uncommon end for old wooden boats. This one can be seen along the McKenzie highway between Leaburg and Vida. Let's make sure we keep using our driftboats, we sure don't want them to end up like this.

continue to be free to enjoy the adventurous challenges of the rivers we must all stand up and take the responsibility to claim our traditions and heritage. If not, the combined knowledge and skills associated with driftboating will go away forever. We must preserve the history and knowledge associated with driftboats. We must restore our fisheries. We must work to establish a system that is equitable to both professional and

This picture was taken during an annual event on the McKenzie River known as the Whitewater Parade. It took place the last Sunday before Opening Day for fishing in May. It continued until it got too big and out of hand, too many rubber duckies, too much alcohol, and rowdies made it too dangerous.

COURTESY OF KENNY KING

The whitewater pram is another modified driftboat manufactured by several builders. It has a squared bow like a Rapid Robert and a partially squared transom bow like the a modern McKenzie driftboat. It is usually built not more than twelve feet long and often it is much shorter. The guys that have them like the light car-topper that can also handle white water.

recreational users of the users of the resource. We must look out for the rights of both riverfront property owners and the public. We must work to take back and keep local control of our rivers. Once the federal government gets control, our voice gets mighty small. There could come a time that you will have to pay a fee or wait in line to enjoy any of our rivers, including the Deschutes, Rogue, Clackamas, or McKenzie. Congress originally stipulated that our western rivers were to remain as highways, free to all of us. I do not recall ever having a voice in turning the rivers into private treasure troves set aside for only those of extraordinary means. Demand accountability now. Demand it from your elected officials, and demand it from the BLM and USFS. Remind them, gently at first, more forcefully if need be, we are their employers. They work for us and have a job responsibility to look out for our interests. If you love floating in a driftboat, then stand up to the real challenge.

As you spend time on the river, take the time to reflect on the men who went before you. The men who developed the boat and figured out how to move it in sync with the river. Join with other users who treasure our great outdoors and the rivers through which they run. Let your voice be heard as you fight to protect our right to enjoy them in as natural and

unspoiled a state as possible. Work for harmony among the various users of the river with a mind towards preserving as much freedom as you can for our descendants.

I wish you the best of times on the river, I hope to see you there. Remember: Become one with your oars and the river. Go with the flow.

Releasing a wild summer steelhead on Michigan's Au Sable River.

Glossary

Anchor: Weighted device made to hold a boat in place to prevent drifting. Drifting could be due to currents, tides or even the wind. The best whitewater anchor is a pyramid or ball-type without flukes or hooks of any kind that could hang up on below-surface structures in the current.

Attitude: The position of the boat in the water. A proper attitude might have your boat in line with the current and facing downstream especially in big waves.

Backferry: Backferry refers to rowing backwards to pull the boat away from obstacles or to pull the boat back towards a specific point. A backferry can be used to pull your boat across the current when moving from one side of the river to the other. A backferry seldom will exceed a 45-degree angle to the current.

Bateau(x): Bateau is the French word for boat. Adding the x changes the singular bateau to the plural.

Big Water: Generally deep, fast, turbulent water. Huge waves, up to ten feet high or higher. Boats here, even under control, can look and feel like little toys being tossed about in a bathtub occupied by a rambunctious child. This kind of water is found on the Colorado, the Snake, and to a lesser degree on the Deschutes during normal flows. It can be found on many rivers during high water (near or above normal flood stage).

Boils: Upwelling of water usually found along eddy lines and irregular cliffs where the current is swift and strong and the water deep and turbulent. This water can be tricky to maneuver or row in and severe boils and whirlpools could combine to capsize your boat.

Boulder Garden: A boulder-choked piece of water requiring expert maneuvering through very technical water. Blossom Bar on the Rogue River is a classic example of a boulder garden.

Bow: The front of the boat. On a driftboat, the front of the boat is whichever end the owner or operator wants to call it. Technically the driftboat travels downstream stern first, but practically speaking the pointed end of the contemporary boat or even the Rapid Robert boat is the bow. See Chapter Four: The Contemporary Driftboat.

Bow Down: Term used by the McKenzie guides that means to turn your bow downstream to row backwards toward the downstream destination. Row downstream rowboat style. This method is used when the oarsman wants to make time moving downstream.

Bow Line: Short tag or tie-off line attached to the bow.

Bow Out: Term used by the McKenzie guides that refers to spinning the boat around an obstacle that otherwise could not be avoided, (also cartwheeling)

Bow Stem: See "Stem."

Broach: A situation where the boat has hung up on an obstruction, often sideways to the current, and is pinned there by that current. There is the danger of the upstream end or side of the boat being sucked under water, consequently sinking the boat.

Carabiner: A metal ring, usually found in the shape of a "D," a pear, or an oval. They have a gate that is usually spring-loaded and can have a threaded lock nut to ensure that they stay closed. In boating applications they are used for attaching tie-off lines, rigging for heavy pulls in a rescue or recovery operation. (See "Z-drag" in Chapter Ten: Trouble on the Water)

CFS (cubic feet per second): The volume of water moving downstream is measured in CFS.

Channel: The part of the river that is a path of water flowing downstream. In any given stretch there may be many channels or as few as only one.

Chine: Chine is the seam that joins the hull and the bottom of the boat. Wood and aluminum boats usually run a channel-type trim around the seam. Fiberglass boats are usually reinforced at this point with extra layers of fabric and resin, but have no real seam as the material is continuos.

Chute: A constricted channel that is fairly narrow in relation to the main body of water. Chutes are usually fast little drops. Sometimes chutes are the only passage that you will find through a rock or boulder garden.

Cushion: The mass of water that stacks up against an obstacle that is extending above the water line. It is a back-flow off the obstacle.

Curler: A standing wave that crests and breaks back over on itself, or the upstream wave or curlback in a reversal. It can mark a big hole or be a fairly benign standing tail wave.

Current: The flow of water, the strength of which is determined by the gradient and volume of the flow.

Dory (Boat): A distant cousin to the driftboat which has a similar profile but only superficial similarities. The main difference between the two boats is the dory has a more narrow hull bottom which allows it to draw more water (have a greater draft). This causes the dory to ride deeper in the water to provide more stability against wind and tide as it is used chiefly in the ocean.

Draft: The depth of the boat beneath the water line. To

measure draft, simply measure from the water line to the deepest part of the hull bottom.

Double-Ender: The McKenzie driftboat designed by Woodie Hindman that came about as a result of Woodie getting turned around in big water in his Rapid Robert. He liked the way the pointed bow cut the big waves without having to "turn a corner" as was needed in the old square-ender. The resulting design was accomplished by extending the lines of the stern of the Rapid Robert out to a point.

Drop: A significant lowering of the river's surface altitude measured over any distance. Usually in terms of river-running, the gradient of the river or the amount of vertical descent in a falls or a rapid.

Dry Bag: Bags made to keep clothes and equipment dry on whitewater river trips. They are commonly made of hypalon, vinyl, and lined nylon.

Dry Boxes: Dry boxes are usually made of aluminum, they have waterproof hinges and seals and watertight latches. There are also some nice plastic dry boxes that are a little less expensive that have recently hit the market.

Eddy: A flow of water opposite of the main current creating a circular motion of water. Examples could be an extreme whirlpool strong enough to sink a driftboat, a back-flow downstream of a small above-surface rock or obstruction, or a huge lazy section of deep slow water that you sometimes find on a big slow bend of the river. Normally, the deeper the pool and the slower the current, the less dangerous an eddy will be. The volume of flow, the speed of the main current, the presence of a deep pool, and the geological formations along the banks and bottom of the river, all contribute to what form the eddy takes.

Eddy Line/Fence: A distinctive band of boily water that marks the boundary between water moving upstream from water moving downstream. It is not unusual for there to be a marked difference in surface level of the water between the upstream and downstream flows of water.

Entrapment: The pinning of a person in rocks or debris on a river. Without immediate help, entrapment is almost always fatal.

Entry: The beginning of a predetermined route through a rapid. The entry may be a rock gate and/or a well-defined "V" pointing your way.

Falls: Either in a steep cascade or free falling, an abrupt vertical drop, as the river dives over a cliff, ledge, or boulder mass. Multnomah Falls and Willamette Falls are free falling. White, Garter Falls, Rainy and Wapinita are Cascade Falls.

Flat Water: Water without rapids or big waves. (unclasssed)

Fluke: The hook on an anchor.

Forward: The front half of the boat.

Freeboard: The portion of the side of the boat that is above water.

Frog Water: Slow, often deep, flat water that will require you to row if you want to get anywhere soon.

Galloway Position: The rowing position pioneered by Nathaniel Galloway during the last decade of the 1800s. In this position the oarsman faces downstream and rows backwards (backferrys) to avoid obstacles. Originally the stern of the boat was always pointed down stream, but in the days of our contemporary driftboats, we call that pointed stern the bow, and that is the part of the boat that travels downstream first.

Gasping Reflex: When a human being is suddenly thrown into very cold water he will have that tendency to immediately and involuntarily gasp for air. This of course results in instant drowning. The best remedy is to be aware that it can happen and consciously fight that reflex. The more time spent swimming the better your chances for surviving this potential risk.

Gate: A narrow passage way that is generally navigated as safe passage, often the entrance to a rapid or particular stretch of river.

Gradient: The drop in surface altitude of a river. It is generally measured in footage of decrease per river mile, i.e., This river drops about 78 feet per mile.

Gunwale: (pronounced gunnel). The upper edge of the side of a boat.

Haystack: A large standing wave. It may be created by an under-the-surface obstacle or by fast-moving water colliding with slow water.

Heavy Water: Deep turbulent water with great big waves and very strong hydrodynamic forces at work. Good examples are Colorado and Rattlesnake rapids on central Oregon's Deschutes river.

Hogback: A rock ledge partially or fully submerged that can cause a boater some concern or difficulty.

Hog Trough: A hole or reversal that is big enough to give you some difficulty if you hit it.

Hole: A hole is a drop over a boulder or ledge just above a reversal. The deeper the drop, the bigger the reversal.

Hydraulic: An adjective transformed by river people into a noun used to name extreme turbulence, with powerful hydrostatic pressure, created when a high volume of water is funneled into a narrow passage with a good-sized drop. Extreme river features such as reversals, boils and whirlpools, large irregular waves, and severe side currents are the kinds of extreme turbulence called *hydraulics*.

Hypothermia: A medical condition defined as a lowering of the body's core temperature. Mild cases are common with river runners, they usually experience symptoms of mental confusion and fatigue. Severe hypothermia, a body temperature of less than 90 degrees, results in a slowing of the heart and breathing rates accompanied by a reduction in blood flow to the extremities. It can be fatal. River-runners should be familiar with how to handle someone with hypothermia.

Jam Cleat: A cleat of metal or plastic used to secure and anchor line in the boat.

Jump Highside: (Rafter's term) When a collision into an obstacle is imminent, move towards the downstream end or side of the boat to give lift to the upstream end or side to help prevent the water from pouring over the side as it is sucked under by the current.

Keeper: A reversal that is strong enough to hold boats or swimmers for a measurable period of time. Often keepers will look quite innocent but have the potential to be extremely dangerous. They are found immediately below cross-current ledges and low head dams where there is a large-volume flow. Do not be deceived by the relatively small backcurler found at low head dams. It is the large, even volume of water that gives them their power.

Ledge: A geologic strata that can run either parallel or at any degree up to perpendicular to the current. A ledge with a hollow underneath that is only partially perpendicular to the current can be a trap for swimmers. Ledges, mixed with water speed and a high volume or CFS and big drops, can be responsible for extreme hydraulics.

Line (Lining): These words have dual meaning in common use on the river. To most rivermen, line means, to lower your boat down a bad section of water by means of tag lines or ropes. Also, rope is referred to as a line.

Log-Driving Bateau(x): Boats developed in the Penebscot River region of Maine for use in the logging industry. They were 23 to 36 feet long and rowed by up to six men. In shallow upstream water, pikers did they're part to help push the heavily laden boats to the logging camps. Coming downstream they were used to herd the logs down to the mill.

Narrows: A section of river marked by constricted passage, frequently caused by narrow channels among steep cliffs. It is not uncommon for narrows to have deeper water than the average river depth. Narrows can be scary, especially if they are long and you must ship your oars. Once those oars are in, all you can do is fasten your seatbelts (PFDs) and hang on for the ride (or dear life).

Pillow: A pillow is a mound of water caused by a boulder laying just below the surface. If the boulder is deep enough, your boat can slide harmlessly over the top, if it's not, the banging on the bottom of your hull will get your attention.

Pool: A section of river that is usually deeper and slower than the average of that river. In Oregon's Cascade rivers, pools separate stretches of fast rock-strewn rapids.

Portage: To carry your gear and boat around an unrunnable section of water.

Portegee: Rowing forward in the direction you are facing.

Pour-Over Rock: Often preceding a hole or reversal, pour-overs are generally a noticeable drop over a fair-sized rock with a good flow of water. Sometimes these are found in the midst of a rapid and sometimes they are the only hazard on an otherwise friendly stretch of river.

Put-In: The place you put your boat into the water. It can be an official boat launch and ramp, a grassy bank, or a cliff that requires you to use a rope to lower it over.

Rake: Upswept or curved gunwales. The more curve, the more rake. It is the high raked sides of the McKenzie boat that gives it its unique dory-like silhouette.

Rapid: A definable section of river usually marked by an obvious drop, turbulent whitewater, and standing waves, or sometimes by a fairly benign drop followed by standing tail waves. Often a dangerous section of river, rapids can be filled with hazards and obstacles like rocks, holes, and strainers. They are a lot of fun to run. You had best know what you are doing if you are in a driftboat on anything more than a Class I.

Rapid Robert: The square-ended original McKenzie River boat perfected by Tom Kaarhus. It was known as the Rapid Robert everywhere but along the McKenzie.

Reversal: Also known as: holes, keepers, white eddies, etc. A river feature that occurs after a sudden drop over a rock, ledge, or even a tree. As the falling water, its speed increased by the drop, meets the slower water below, a wave is created that breaks back over itself. This creates an upstream or reverse flow of water. Reversals can be sized from so tiny as to be barely noticeable with no effect on a boat to giants that can flip a boat as though it were a child's toy in a bath tub.

Riffle: A rapid too small to be rated. Riffles usually are very shallow with small choppy waves over gravel bottoms. Careful planning and judgment in choosing which and where the deepest channel lays will save you some time dragging and pulling your boat back into water deep enough to float it.

River-Driving Bateau(x): Smaller versions of the log-driving bateaux that were used to ferry men and equipment on small-scale rivers. (See Zane Grey's boat in Chapter Two: Boats of the Rogue River.)

River Velocity: The speed of the current. The average speed of the current in rivers is about 5 MPH or less but speeds of 10 MPH or so can be reached through a rapid.

River Flow: The volume of water currently moving downstream. This is generally measured in CFS—cubic feet per second.

Rock Garden: A section of river choked with rocks, usually smaller than those found in a boulder garden, but otherwise the same.

Rocker: The curvature of the bottom of the boat is called the rocker. Just like a rocking chair.

Roller: This term usually refers to a large standing wave which is breaking back on itself like an ocean breaker or roller. Sometimes it is used to refer to a large wave in a reversal. See "Curler" and "Standing Wave."

Rooster Tail: Rooster tails are sometimes your first visual indication of an upcoming rapid. As you move closer to the entrance of a rapid the less obvious they become. A rooster tail is first visible as a near vertical plume of water that seams to be shooting skyward off a rock. Actually they are caused by the splash of a curler in a hole.

Shipping: To take on board. Commonly used by driftboaters to refer to taking water on board over the side or pulling in the oars for a tight passage.

Sidecurler: A curler or roller wave that is parallel to the current, These are usually found along irregular cliffs and shoreline rocks in heavy water. Also found on tight or fast outside corners.

Sleeper: A submerged boulder that is unmarked by ripple or wave, but is shallow enough to give you some kind of trouble if you hit it. In fast water, collision with a sleeper could potentially cause you to capsize.

Souse Hole: Souse holes are small reversals. These mini-hydraulics can be strong enough to grab your boat and slow your momentum.

Square-Ender: The original McKenzie River driftboat design as perfected by Tom Kaarhus. Known on other rivers as the Rapid Robert.

Standing Wave: Large waves that are created by the collision of fast water meeting slower water. Sometimes these waves appear, inexplicably to the eye, in the middle of a stream. Most of the time though, you will find standing waves in the tail-end section of a rapid. Here they joyfully dance and frolic while beckoning you to go for a ride. These tailout waves usually offer fairly benign roller-coaster rides.

Stem (Bow Stem): The upright support on the pointed end(s) of a driftboat. See the "Introduction" for a boat diagram.

Stopper: A stopper is a reversal large enough to stop your forward momentum and require you to row down stream with some power.

Strainer: Strainers are one of the most dangerous obstacles on the river. Often strainers look innocent to the untrained eye. This kind of obstacle allows the passage of water, but not objects or people. Strainers are often lethal when they combine with strong currents to catch an unlucky swimmer or boat. The trees described in Chapter Two were strainers and almost the scene of a disaster.

Tail Waves: A row of standing waves found at the end of a rapid when it meets slower waters or empties into a pool. (See photo on page Xx of standing waves. These are tail waves at the bottom of Martin's Creek Rapid on the McKenzie River.)

Take Out: The place you take your boat out of the water, be it boat ramp, steep muddy bank, or a pole slide.

Technical Water: Water that is strewn with boulders and other obstacles which require you to make many course changes in order to negotiate them. Martin's Creek rapid on the McKenzie river is considered to be technical water, in fact, the whole upper McKenzie is. So is Blossom Bar Rapid on the Rogue.

Tongue: A "V" caused by water flowing past a couple of obstructions which points downstream. It is usually smoother, darker water and often marks the safest entry point to a rapid.

Transom: The flat end of a boat as opposed to the pointed end. Transoms are often used as a motor mount.

Trash Head: Lazy, irresponsible people that leave trash wherever they go, particularly along rivers and in camp spaces.

Trim: Trim is a nautical term that describes balancing the load in your vessel. You want it to ride evenly not listing to one side or the other.

Trough: The area between two standing or curling waves. It could also refer to a hole in the front of a reversal.

V Slick: A tongue marking a downstream channel when pointing downstream. The marker of a rock or other obstacle when pointing upstream.

Wrap(ped): River-runner's term used to describe a boat getting wrapped around a mid-stream rock.

White Eddy: An aerated (whitewater) eddy usually found downstream from an above-surface obstacle.

Yaw: To sway back and forth in the current when anchored in fast water.

Bibliography

The Rogue: A River To Run. Florence Arman. Wildwood Press. Grants Pass, Oregon. 1982.

Guide To Floating Whitewater Rivers. R. W. Miskimins. Frank Amato Publications. Portland, Oregon. 1987.

Whitewater Rafting. William McGinnis. Random House. New York, New York. 1975.

Driftboater's Guide To The Upper McKenzie. Doc Crawford. Northwest Rivers Publishing Inc. Eugene, Oregon. 1986.

Steelhead Drift Fishing. Bill Luch. Frank Amato Publications. Portland, Oregon. 1976.

Handbook To The Rogue River Canyon. James A. Quinn, James W. Quinn, James G. King. Frank Amato Publications. Portland, Oregon. 1978.

Handbook To The Deschutes River Canyon. James A. Quinn, James W. Quinn, James G. King. Frank Amato Publications. Portland, Oregon. 1979.

River Rescue. Les Bechdel and Slim Ray. Appalachian Mountain Club Books. Boston, Massachusetts. 1989.

Wilderness And Travel Medicine. Eric A. Weiss, MD. Adventure Medical Kits. Oakland, California. 1997.

First Through The Grand Canyon: The Expedition Of Major John Wesley Powell. Steve Frazee. Holt, Rinehart and Winston. New York, New York. 1961.

Fishing In Oregon. Madelynn Diness Sheehan and Dan Casali. Frank Amato Publications. Portland, Oregon. 1995.

The Big Drops: Ten Legendary Rapids. Robert O. Collins and Roderick Nash. The Sierra Club. 1978.

The Doing Of The Thing: The Brief Brilliant Whitewater Career of Buzz Holmstrom. Vince Welch, Cort Conley, Brad Dimock. Fretwater Press. Flagstaff, Arizona. 1998.

Driftboat Strategies. Neale Streeks. Pruett Publishing Company. Boulder, Colorado. 1997.

The Trailblazers. Bil Gilbert. Time/Life Books. Alexandria, Virginia. 1979.

Articles

"Where There's A Willie There's A Way." Bill Monroe. *Portland Oregonian.* February 11, 1993.

"The Boat The McKenzie River Spawned." Jim Boyd. *Eugene Register-Guard.* December 14, 1975.

"The McKenzie River Driftboat." John Babbs. *Wooden Boat Magazine.* Issue Number 52.

"Maritime and Aviation Consultants." Craig Lynch, Associate. *Expert Newsletter,* Fall 1991. Website address: http://macexperts.com/macnewsletters/fall91/accidents_involving_driftboats.htm

Index

Boat Builders

Alumaweld Boats Inc.
2000 Rogue River Drive
Eagle Point, OR 97524
541-826-7171
www.alumaweldboats.com

Clackamas Marine
13111 S.E. Highway 212
Clackamas, OR 97015
800-394-1345
www.clacka.com

Fish-Rite Boats
1419 Justice Road
Central Point, OR 97502
541-776-0621
www.fish-right.com

Don Hill Custom River Boats
6690 McKenzie River Highway
Springfield, OR 97478
541-747-7430
www.dhdriftboats.com

Koffler Boats
90017 Greenhill Road
Eugene, OR 97402
541-688-6093

Lavro, Inc.
16311 177 Avenue S.E.
Monroe, WA 98272
888-337-2980
fax: 360-794-5525
sales@lavroboats.com

Motion Marine
22768 S. Johnson Road
West Linn, OR 97219
888-290-1802
www.motionmarine.com

Ray's River Dories
3839 S.W. Multnomah
Portland, OR 97219
503-244-3608

Willie Boats
1440 Justice Road
Central Point, OR 97502
800-866-7775/ fax: 541-779-9346
www.willieboats.com/hwillie.html

Wooldridge Boats
9224 Martin Luther King Jr. Way S.
Seattle, WA 98118
203-722-8998
wooldridged@uswest.nat

Modeling

Don Hill Custom Boats
6690 McKenzie River Highway
Springfield, OR 97478
541-747-7430
www.dhdriftboats.com

The River's Touch
2353 East Ellendale
Dalles, OR 97338
503-623-0638
www.riverstouch.com

Government Agencies

U.S. Department of Agriculture
(U.S. Forest Service)
P.O. Box 96090
Washington DC 20090-690
202-205-1760

U.S. Forest Service
(contact the regional office
for your area)

Regional Ecosystem Office
(U.S. Forest Service in Oregon)
333 S.W. First
Portland, Oregon
503-808-2165

**Department of the Interior
Bureau of Land Management**
1849 C Street N. W,
Washington DC 20038
Mail Stop 406 L Street
202-452-5125
www.blm.gov

**U.S. National Park Service
Headquarters**
"C" Street, NW
Washington, DC 20240
202-208-6843
www.nps.gov

Oregon State Marine Board
P.O. Box 14145
Salem, Oregon 97309-5065
503-378-8587

Groups and Associations

American Canoe Association
7432 Alban Station Boulevard
Springfield, VA 22150-2311
703-451-0141
acadirect@aol.com

American Rivers
1025 Vermont Avenue N.W.
Suite 720
Washington, DC 20005
202-347-7550

American Whitewater Affiliation
1430 Fenwick Lane
Silver Spring, MD 20910
301-589-9453
www.awa.org

**Grand Canyon
Private Boaters Association**
(GCPBA)
P.O. Box 2133
Flagstaff, AZ 86003-2133
520-214-8676
www.flagstaff.com

**McKenzie River
Guides Association**
P.O. Box 1002
Leaburg, OR 97489
800-832-5858

National Organization of Rivers
212 W. Cheyenne Mountain
Boulevard
Colorado Springs, CO 80906-3712
719-379-8759

Northwest Rafters Association
10117 S.E. Sunnyside Road, F1234
Clackamas, OR 97015
www.teleport.com/~nwra

Northwest Steelheaders
6641 S.E. Lake Road
Milwaukie, OR 97222
503-653-4176

Oregon Kayak and Canoe
P.O. Box 692
Portland, OR 97206
360-882-6502

Oregon Guides and Packers
P.O. Box 673
Springfield, OR 97477
541-937-3192
ogpsue@msn.com

Wild Wilderness
248 N.W. Wilmington Avenue
Bend, OR 97701
541-385-5261
ssilver@wildwilderness.org

Willamette Kayak and Canoe
P.O. Box 1062
Corvalis, OR 97339
541-753-3406
ndp@oce.orst.edu

DAN ALSUP, A NATIVE OF PORTLAND, OREGON, LIVES WITH HIS WIFE, Donna. They have four children; Rachael, Nathan, Danielle and Bridget.

Dan is an avid outdoorsman and student of Oregon history with a great passion for wild rivers, boating and fishing. He practically cut his teeth on the banks of the Clackamas River camping and fishing with his parents. The upper Clackamas River also provided his first whitewater experience when he was about fourteen years old, igniting a love of river adventuring. Alsup says, "A perfect day would have to include running some whitewater and steelhead fishing."

Dan is a contractor and occasionally guides fishing and rafting trips. He has been a member of both the Oregon Guides and Packers Association (now known as Oregon Outdoors) and a Northwest Rafters Association.